KIDS
FOR
KEEPS

KIDS FOR KEEPS

Preventing Injuries to Children

Martin Lesperance

Kids for Keeps Ltd.
Cochrane, Alberta

July 1995

The author and publisher of the book have checked with sources believed to be reliable in a conscientious effort to provide information that is complete and congruent with acceptable standards at the time of this publication. However, the dynamic nature of this information leads us to anticipate future changes and updates. Therefore, readers are encouraged to confer with other reliable sources to ensure that they will receive complete, accurate and current information.

Cover illustration by Calvin Pinder

Canadian Cataloguing in Publication Data

Lesperance, Martin, 1953-
Kids for Keeps

ISBN 0-9698989-0-8

Includes bibliographical references and index.

1. Children's accidents-Prevention. 2. Safety education. I. Title.
HV675.72.L47 1995   363.1'0083   C95-910131-4

Printed in Edmonton, Alberta, Canada by Art Design Printing Inc.
Typesetting, layout & design by Satoo Design & Graphics Inc.

Dedication

To my wife Shelley, who put up with my passion for this book, and to my daughters Chloe and Caida who made me realize just how precious children are.

To my Mom who raised me safely, but still allowed me the freedom to explore and to seek adventure.

Children are a gift from God;
they are a real blessing.

Psalm 127.3

Telephone Numbers

POLICE DEPARTMENT	
FIRE DEPARTMENT	
AMBULANCE	
POISON CONTROL	
EMERGENCY	
HOSPITAL	
FAMILY DOCTOR	
PEDIATRICIAN	
DAY CARE CENTRE	
BABY SITTER	

Table of Contents

Acknowledgements

I would like to thank Dr. Wadeia Yacoub from the Capital Health Authority, formally the City of Edmonton Board of Health for his time, knowledge and resources. I would also like to thank him for his permission to reproduce the cartoons and information from the newsletters that are produced by the Edmonton Board of Health.

Thank you to my wife, Shelley and to her mother Dorothy Stanley who did much of the initial editing. Also to my daughter Chloe who became my research assistant, Kathy Belton of the University of Alberta Injury Prevention Centre for her time and comments when reviewing my manuscript; to Carol Sheehan for assistance with editing.

A special thanks to Donna Hastings for reviewing the material in my manuscript, her many suggestions have been most helpful. Thanks to Jan Langill for many of the case histories.

Thanks to Bob Long of Satoo Design & Graphics Inc. for his patience and understanding when I changed my mind so often, and to Bernd Gretzinger for the encouragement.

Introduction

If a disease were killing our children in the proportions that accidents are, people would be outraged and demand that this killer be stopped (Everett Koop, M.D., ScD., Chairman, National SAFE KIDS Campaign).

A t one time disease was the principal cause of death among children. However, with the advent of modern medicine and highly effective vaccines, disease doesn't kill nearly as many children as do injuries from so-called accidents.

When I started working in the Emergency Medical Services as a paramedic, I dealt with many seriously injured people. Some of those people died as a result of their injuries; some of them were children. When a child died, that death affected me and my co-workers in a different way than when an adult died. It was always the calls about injured and dying children that seemed to stay in my memory. I was responding to calls concerning injured children before I became a parent myself. I used to think that I could empathize with parents of injured or dying children, but I never realized I could love someone as much as I love my children. Becoming a parent has made me realize the anguish parents go through when a child is injured. So now when I attend those situations where children are injured, I do not say to the parents, "I know how you must feel." The truth is, I have never been through what those parents are going through, but calls regarding injured children affect me even more now that I'm a parent than they did before. I have not only worked as a paramedic, but I have also spent many years designing and instruct-

*In the interest of simplicity, the pronouns his/her and he/she are used interchangeably. Discrimination is not a factor when emergencies occur.

ing First Aid courses for many different industries. Very often during these courses the subject would turn to dealing with injured children. Eventually I decided to design a First Aid program dealing specifically with children. When I began to work on my program, this question occurred to me: *Why not try to prevent injuries from happening to children in the first place?* So it was with that question that I began this book. I truly hope that *Kids for Keeps* will make people aware of the hazards to be found around the house, and that it will help people to take action to eliminate those hazards. Eliminating hazards should reduce the chance of your child experiencing a serious injury. Every year thousands of children are killed or injured in accidents, and most of those "accidents" could have been anticipated and most of the injuries could have been prevented. Every child will experience bumps and bruises; that is part of growing up. However, with a few safety procedures and some knowledge of the kinds of injuries that have happened to other children, you can reduce the chance of serious injury to your child. *Kids for Keeps* attempts to share some of that knowledge with you. It would be impossible to list every dangerous situation that your child could encounter. What I would like to do is instill in you an awareness of potential hazards in your home. That awareness should keep you alert to dangers in your home from the time you bring your children home from the hospital until they are old enough to make safe decisions on their own. If you can look at things from a child's viewpoint and try to anticipate the dangerous situations that await your child, you are well on your way to preventing injuries to your children. We cannot expect children to live in a plastic bubble, but we can work to limit some of the dangers that they will encounter.

About the Book

This book begins with some of the common hazards that

can be found in your child's environment. It is amazing how many unusual ways children can find to injure themselves. The first part of this book deals with very general hazards. The next section of the book discusses more specific hazards to be found in different areas of the house, yard, and garage. Next, day care settings, baby-sitters, and other substitute caregivers are discussed. There are special hazards to consider when parents are not available. Playing outdoors with your child is a joy, but it brings with it special safety concerns. The chapter on the outdoors is followed by chapters that deal with motor vehicles, bicycles, and recreational equipment and vehicles. Various other chapters deal with safety in rural settings, safety with toys, and holiday safety. A final chapter summarizes the book's most important points. It will teach your child about personal safety and will teach you what to do if your child is missing. While you are probably aware of many of the hazards that are mentioned in the book and you can use common sense or conventional wisdom to eliminate them, there may be others that have never crossed your mind. Sometimes you will find repetition in certain chapters. I have intentionally repeated important basic principles in case you elect to read specific sections of the book rather than read it cover to cover. This book was compiled from many sources, using the most current information possible. I have included a bibliography and a reference section in the back of the book with suggestions for further reading. Many of the incidents that I have mentioned in this book are actual ambulance calls I have responded to. I have included these because I believe that adults, like children, learn by example. My experience as a paramedic has given me insights into how injury prevention can save lives. In the field, the rules of safety become a concrete reality; failure to follow the rules can result in tragedy. I hope that my experiences will alert you to potential hazards in your child's environment and that they will make you pause to think about the potential consequences of seemingly innocent actions.

George Bernard Shaw once wrote: Perhaps the greatest social service that can be rendered by anybody to the country and to mankind is to bring up a family.

I believe that in order to bring up our children, we need to provide a safe and healthy environment in which they can grow and thrive. Kids are for keeps.

Martin Lesperance, 1995

The Growing Child

1

C hildren require different kinds of protection at different ages; that is, there are specific safety needs for each age. A general observation for all age groups is that injuries are caused by two things: unsafe actions and unsafe conditions. In this chapter, I will review some of the developmental stages of early childhood and indicate some of the hazards associated with each one. Keep in mind, however, that no two children are the same. Your child is unique. You may need different safety measures for your child's environment than the parents next door need for their children. This chapter is designed to assist you in assessing safety measures appropriate for your child, and alert you to those safety tips which apply to *all young children.*

I have included some statistics from the Canadian Institute of Child Health (CICH) book, *The Health of Canada's Children* (second edition, 1994). Some of the statistics are surprising; all of them should impress on us the many dangers to children that we can help eliminate through attention to safety. Some of the more common ways that children are injured are these:

- Motor vehicle collisions;
- Falls, either from being dropped, or from rolling off surfaces;
- Choking on food or small objects;
- Suffocation and strangulation;
- Drowning;
- Burns and scalds.

The danger of injuries is always greatest at times of stress or during changes in routine. Here are some danger times to be aware of. You should take extra care during these unusual periods to reduce the chance of injury to your child:

- Just before mealtimes, when everyone is hungry and tired;

- When someone in the family is ill;

- When you are moving from one house or apartment to another;

- When you are in a hurry;

- When you have visitors.

1. Birth to Four Months

Suffocation is the leading cause of injury death for babies under 1 year, accounting for one third of the total. More than half (57%) of these suffocation deaths are due to mechanical causes, and one third are due to food. Motor vehicle accidents account for a further 20% of deaths. (CICH, 1994:23)

Newborns are totally reliant on your care and protection. From the time of their birth until infants are about four months old, their primary occupations are eating and sleeping, and, of course, having their diapers changed. There will be crying connected to these events — probably more than first-time parents could anticipate. Even in the first few weeks, newborns can wriggle about. They will spend a lot of time in the crib reaching for things, swinging their little arms and kicking their little legs. At around four months children will probably be rolling over unassisted, putting objects into their mouths and pulling things over their face. Do not think that they cannot get into trouble at this young age; they can, and they will try.

2. Five to Seven Months

At approximately five months, infants will start to be more mobile. Rolling around in the crib and on the floor will be great sport for them. At this age they have figured out what hands are for, and they will grab onto anything that is within their reach. Whatever is grasped will be put into their mouths. At around six months, they will learn to sit up unassisted, and before you know it they might even be crawling. At approximately seven months is when real trouble can begin to happen.

At this age injuries are often caused by falls from furniture, tumbles down stairs, motor vehicle collisions, and poisonings. In addition, children may suffer burns from exploring electrical outlets, or from investigating water and heat sources. Supervision is therefore essential. Many injuries may be prevented if you examine your child's environment, anticipate what type of trouble your child will be able to get into, and take precautions before a dangerous situation occurs. When you ask yourself whether your baby's world is safe, also ask whether you are changing to meet the needs of this increasingly active little person.

> *The leading cause of injury hospitalization for babies is falls — they account for 30% of all admissions due to injury. (CICH, 1994:33)*

3. Eight to Twelve Months

Children grow rapidly from eight to twelve months and at this stage of development they are able to pull themselves up into a standing position. They are incredibly curious. That means, for example, that they will be able to reach things on coffee tables all by themselves. Teething discomfort is sometimes relieved by chewing and biting all sorts of things. You need to be vigilant.

Language skills are beginning to develop at this age and your baby will begin to understand some common words when those words are accompanied with gestures. The child will try to mimic your sounds and words. Babies can respond to some simple commands and are beginning to learn the meaning of "no."

The safety practices you have already been practicing still apply, but you need to supplement them with new ones. As your child becomes increasingly mobile, your concerns for safety should multiply almost daily. This is when you need to get down on your own hands and knees and view your environment from the vantage point of your crawling child. Child-proofing can prevent injuries, and an awareness of your baby's new physical abilities can help you plan safety measures.

Babies' motor skills are far from perfect and they are at high risk for injuries at this stage. At this age injuries are usually caused by falls, burns from a variety of sources, and motor vehicle collisions. Drowning, suffocation, and poisoning are also common at this age. Children at this age will put anything into their mouths, and because they are quite mobile, they find more things to put into their mouths. Strict attention must be paid to what types of plants you have, and to where you store your medications, cleaning materials, and other toxic substances. No doubt you will have done this kind of inventory and secured these hazards behind locked doors before your child was born. By this point, keeping these things safely away from your child should be almost second nature to you.

4. Twelve to Twenty-four Months

Between twelve and eighteen months your child will learn to walk unassisted. These are the "toddler" months and the time when children become independent explorers. Curiosity is the order of the day; getting into things is their way of learning about the world around them. Experimentation, seeing how things work, and doing activities "by myself" are the hallmarks of this stage of development.

The child's development of language is marked by the understanding of simple statements and questions, and an increasing vocabulary. After about eighteen months, toddlers will begin using some two-word sentences, will learn to ask for favorite objects by name, and begin to understand simple directions. Generally children understand more words than they can speak.

As they begin to talk, toddlers will start to imitate adults. This is a very good time for parents, siblings, other relatives, and other caregivers to set a good example for children. Practicing safety is a way of teaching safety.

Close supervision is of paramount importance at this age — in and out of the house. Toddlers can move quickly, and it takes only a very short time for them to travel into danger, which is a concept that they haven't acquired yet. They are still too young to learn from experience, and they will often repeat an activity that has already resulted in an injury. Without supervision, toddlers easily get into trouble as they explore and climb to unbelievable heights, just out of curiosity! Doors must be secured to prevent children from escaping or falling down stairs. Poisoning is an especially high hazard with this age group.

In 1990, almost 225 preschoolers died as a result of injuries. For every child who died, there were 75 admissions to hospital for injuries. It is also estimated that a further 1,000 children sought medical attention. (CICH, 1994:53)

5. Twenty-four Months and Older

The preschooler is three to four years of age. Children at this stage of development love exploring and playing outside, especially with other children of their own age. They are growing stronger and they are able to ride tricycles, play rough games, and climb on monkey bars. They run, climb, and jump from varying heights. In these early years especially, "vertically challenged" doesn't seem to be part of children's vocabulary. They

Of the 559 preschoolers who died in 1990, 40% died from injuries.... Injury deaths accounted for about twice as many deaths as birth defects and four times as many as cancer. (CICH, 1994:44)

Boys are more likely to die than girls — in fact, almost twice as many preschool boys die than girls. (CICH, 1994:53)

are quickly becoming more independent, a phenomenon that seemingly increases with age. Their independence is sometimes different from their ability or willingness to understand what you are saying. In other words, the "selective hearing" of this age group can be frustrating for parents and caregivers. Despite "selective hearing," however, preschoolers develop linguistically from being able to follow simple two-step directions to being able to carry out three related directions. They speak clearly and with increasing accuracy, and form increasingly complex complete sentences. They can follow and give directions, and they can give reasons, answers, and descriptions of objects and events.

At this stage of development children are very teachable. It is time to start teaching them how to play safely: what and whom they can play with; where to play; and what they can and should not touch. Even though they may learn these safety concepts, children may not always remember them. Though preschoolers are more aware of danger than toddlers, and though they have increased motor, emotional, and cognitive skills, their ideas about cause and effect are still far from perfect. Without practiced reasoning skills to anticipate and understand the dangers they can get into, these children are still at risk from a multitude of hazards. Parents, therefore, must continue the safety measures they used during the earlier years of toddlerhood, and even babyhood. Be patient, set an example, and practice safety at all times.

Over the 5-year period 1986 to 1990, 424 preschoolers died as a result of motor vehicle accidents, 191 preschoolers drowned and 187 died as a result of burns. Motor vehicle collisions account for 38% of all injury deaths. Drownings account for 17% of all injury deaths. (CICH, 1994:45)

It is at the preschool age that we can begin to see the truth in the old adage "a child's work is his or her play." It is our work as parents and guardians of children to see that their play is done safely. As is true of any age, if children are left alone, and have not been taught the fundamentals of safety, they will find a way to get into trouble. If we have not made that environment safe for children, the trouble that could result could be tragically catastrophic. Supervision is crucial to preventing injuries: never leave a child without supervision.

Grim as they are, the statistics have an underlying logic and lessons for us to learn. Injuries can happen anywhere and the dangers in this world for children are frightening. It is up to us as parents and caregivers to know something about the kind and incidence of injuries occurring at given age levels so that we can make our child's world safer and, hopefully, injury free. The good news is that we can often anticipate and prevent danger in our children's environment. By eliminating unsafe actions and unsafe conditions we can contribute to a safe and healthy childhood for our children and ensure that our *kids are for keeps.*

Falls   2

As a cause of unintentional deaths, falls are outranked only by deaths due to motor vehicle injuries. Falls account for 40% of all the unintentional deaths in Canadian homes.

Falls are responsible for a great deal of pain and suffering. Falls can happen anywhere: from heights as low the kitchen counter or as great as the garage roof. The results range from minor discomforts such as a skinned knee, to injuries that may be devastating, or even life threatening. For instance, a fall could result in paralysis from the neck down. That sort of injury could hospitalize your child for the rest of his life.

In 1994 in Toronto, a child fell out of a third floor window. When the mother screamed a man who happened to be walking by looked up and caught the baby. The baby was virtually unharmed. Most of us would not be so lucky.

1. Counters and Change Tables

- Never leave a small child unattended on a kitchen or a bathroom counter for "just a second" to answer the phone or to get something. Don't do it: it is frighteningly easy for the child to fall off.

- Never leave a child unattended on a change table. Most change tables have a safety belt on them, but these belts are intended only to restrain an active infant while you are standing next to her. Do not think that because the belt is attached you can leave your child unattended.

2. Balconies and Windows

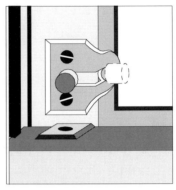

Window Lock

- Railings should be placed along stairs and across balconies to prevent falls. A narrow vertical railing spaced $2^3/_8$ inches (6 cm) or less is recommended.

- Balcony doors should be locked to prevent children from going out alone. Fit balcony railings with guards to prevent a child from squeezing through the rungs or climbing over the top of the railing. A child can squeeze through railings head first, which could result in a disastrous fall; or he can go through feet first, and get his head caught between the rails. This could result in strangulation. Even small children can climb onto balcony furniture, window boxes, or barbecues, and fall over the railing. Railing guards may be purchased from any store which carries child safety products.

- Children have fallen through windows that have been open as little as 5 inches (13 cm). Check elevated windows to make sure they cannot be opened wide enough for a child to crawl through. Don't leave furniture or other things that a child can climb close to a window. Use window locks; most window and sliding glass door locks can be adjusted to permit ventilation.

- Do not rely on window screens to prevent falls; they are often not securely mounted in the window frame, and a child may push out the screen or break through the screen material. Install proper window guards.

3. Home Interiors

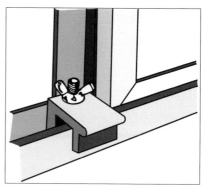

Window Lock

- Corners of objects such as furniture and walls in home interiors present particular hazards if a child loses his balance and falls against them. For example, the corners of coffee tables or the jutting edge of a fireplace hearth. Pads can be purchased that attach to furniture and walls to help protect little heads.

- Pick up tools, shoes, toys, magazines, and other items that shouldn't be left lying about. Pick them up whenever you see them and train children to put their things away.

- Wipe up spills immediately.

- Anchor scatter rugs with rubber matting or an anti-skid coating. Repair and secure curled linoleum, broken or loose tiles, and frayed edges of rugs.

- Poor lighting contributes to falls. In addition to adequate lighting on stairs and in hallways, use night-lights in baseboard outlets in areas that might be navigated late at night.

4. Stairs

Most of us have taken a tumble down a few stairs without serious injury. We were lucky. Each year, according to the U.S. Consumer Product Safety Commission, falls on stairs send more than 750,000 people to the emergency department. I have seen several people who have fallen down only a few stairs, and have broken their neck. Tragically, many of these people become paralyzed for life.

In 1991 a father was carrying his 10 month old child down a long flight of stairs when he tripped on some objects that were on the stairs. He fell forward and down the stairs. He dropped, and then landed on his child. The child suffered two broken legs.

- Ensure all inside and outside stairs are equipped with handrails, and train all members of your family to use them at all times.

- Make sure that you are able to see where you are going while travelling up or down stairs, especially when you are carrying something. Never rush.

- While thick rugs on interior stairs may protect your child to a certain extent in a fall, you must make sure the rugs are well anchored. Loosely anchored runners can increase the possibility of you or the children going for a tumble. Be vigilant: examine carpeted stairs for worn spots that can create trip hazards.

- Experts recommend rubber treads, abrasive strips and skid-resistant paints as the best stair coverings.

- Avoid slippery wax finishes or greasy spots on interior stairs. Keep exterior stairs free of ice, snow, and wet leaves.

- Make sure your stairs are in good condition, and keep them clear of toys or any other things that can trip you. Too often stairs become stacking or storage places for things we want to carry upstairs later.

- Staircase walls filled with pictures may be a dangerous distraction for visitors and small children.

- Do not put a small rug at the top of a set of stairs. A slip on it could result in a tumble down the stairs. Make sure area rugs have a non-slip under-cushion.

- If the open portion of the riser on your stairs has a gap of more than five inches, consider installing acrylic panels on the back of each riser to prevent a child from trapping her head or squeezing through the opening and falling.

5. Safety Gates

Safety gates are devices that can keep small children in or out of a room. If used properly, they are also very useful in limiting access to rooms and stairways.

There are several types of safety gates on the market. Some are made in an accordion style from slats of wood; others are made from a close lace work of plastic strips. Some are held in place in the doorway from pressure exerted on the doorway by the gate. Others are mechanically secured to the door frame with screws. Pressure-mounted gates are not recommended for use in preventing access to stairways; they can give way when leaned on by a child. If the gate were to fail at the top of a set of stairs, the result could be a disastrous fall.

There are cases on record of fatalities caused by older model accordion-style safety gates. Children have squeezed their heads through the openings, resulting in head entrapment and strangulation. Another problem with the older style accordion gate is that the gap at the top of the gate can trap a child's neck. Do not use this type unless it meets *current* safety standards.

There have been situations where ambulances have been called because a parent has tried to step over the gate, tripped, and fallen down the stairs. Take the time to open the gate, pass through, and then securely lock the gate again. Consider the time spent to double check the security of your safety gate as time well spent.

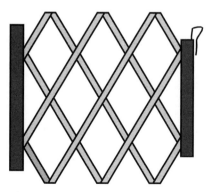

Older Style Safety Gates are Dangerous

- Follow manufacturers' directions for installation.

- If you are mounting the gate with screws, make sure the screws are attached solidly into studs and not just into drywall. The drywall will not secure the gate adequately.

- The gate should be flush with the floor. Don't tempt a child by creating a space she might be able to crawl under. Children have tried to squeeze underneath gates that were not flush to the floor, and have become trapped.

- The gate should not have holds that might encourage a child to try to climb over it.

- Make sure the gate requires a two-step procedure to open. This reduces the chance of the child unintentionally opening it.

- The lock should be on the side away from where the baby usually is, to help prevent unintentional opening.

- The gate should not have any openings larger than $2\frac{3}{8}$ inches (6 cm). This reduces the chance of head and limb entrapment.

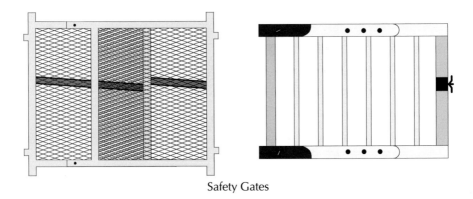

Safety Gates

Baby Danger

6. Baby Walkers

There have been many child injuries attributed to baby walkers. Baby walkers are not safe: they are often unstable and can tip; they can also collapse easily. In addition, a child's tiny fingers can get jammed between the frame of the walker and furniture; and with the assistance of a walker, a child can also reach harmful items that he normally could not reach.

With a baby walker, a child also becomes more mobile than would normally be expected for his age. For example, a child in a walker could travel surprisingly quickly through an open doorway leading to the basement. The door might have been left open for only a moment by a parent, visitor, or sibling. Not only might the child arrive at the open doorway very quickly, but because a child is likely to make the walker top heavy, the child could fall head first down the stairs. Serious, even fatal, head injuries are a common result of this kind of fall.

Some people believe that walkers will help a child learn to walk. *There is no scientific proof to support this assumption. Most experts agree that, purely as a part of normal development, a child will start to walk when she is ready.*

If you do decide to use a baby walker, extreme care must be taken with its use. In addition to increasing the danger of falls, walkers bring the child closer to other dangers such as electrical appliance cords, plants, and other potential hazards. You must be even more vigilant about hazards if your child is using a walker.

Because of their increasing unpopularity with child care experts — **including the *Canadian Medical Association, which recommends that they not be used*** — walkers are difficult to find in stores, but they are often handed down or purchased in garage sales. If you remain unconvinced and despite all the evidence, you still want your child to use a walker, here are some important safety tips for you to follow.

Baby Walker

- You should not use a walker for a child who cannot sit up without assistance.

- You should never leave a child unsupervised in a walker; the baby walker should not be used as a "baby sitter."

- With the increased mobility she has in a walker, your child can get into danger much faster than you can imagine. Using the walker, she can move at a rate of one meter per second.

- When a child is sitting in a walker, he has reaching abilities that he normally would not have.

- A walker should only be used on a floor that is level and clear of objects that could upset it.

- Make sure that the walker will not fit easily through door openings.

- The seat should be equipped with a seat belt that is easy to use.

- The walker should have sturdy construction. Check the walker frequently to be sure that parts are not starting to loosen or break.

- Sometimes older siblings will make a sport of pushing the baby around the house in the walker. Walkers are not go-carts; this practise should be prohibited.

Choking, Suffocation, Strangulation, and Drowning

3

During the four-year period from 1987 and 1991, 1,252 children from the ages of zero to four years old were hospitalized in Alberta due to choking, suffocation, strangulation, and drowning. These alarming figures do not include fatalities. As an emergency paramedic, I have been involved with several drownings, unintentional hangings, and suffocations. In every instance the parents were horrified at how quickly the tragedy occurred. "I just took my eyes off them for a second" was the all-too-common reply when asked what had happened. Injuries involving the blockage of a child's oxygen intake often result in serious injuries, many of them requiring extensive rehabilitation. And very often, these incidents resulted in the death of a child.

You could save a life by knowing how to treat a child who has suffered such an injury, and by taking action before emergency crews arrive. **Take a Cardio-Pulmonary Resuscitation course (CPR) from a recognized agency that meets the guidelines of the Heart and Stroke Foundation of Canada.** Courses in adult, child, and infant CPR are available. However, you should remember that prevention, through the elimination of hazards that cause those situations, is your first step. Here are some ways to eliminate choking, strangulation, suffocation, and drowning situations.

1. Hanging and Head Entrapment

A. Cribs, Playpens, and Other Equipment. (see also the Detailed Discussion in Chapter Seven, The Child's Room.)

- Make sure your crib, playpens, bunk beds, swings, toys, and other equipment for infants and young children conform to the safety standards of the Product Safety Bureau, Health Canada. (Check the Blue Pages of your local phone book for their address.)

- If you borrow a crib or bassinet, make sure it meets the current safety standards. For example, the spacing between the slats and bars on cribs must be no more than $2^{3}/_{8}$ inches (6 cm). The Product Safety Bureau, Health Canada has a brochure on safety standards for cribs.

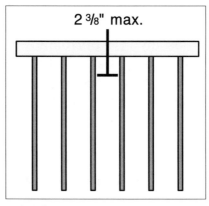

2 ⅜" max.

Crib Sides

- Children have died of strangulation when a button on their clothing has become caught in the mesh sides of a playpen. Strangulation may result when a child trips or falls and her clothing tightens around her throat. In

Canada there are standards governing the size of the holes in the mesh used for playpens; these regulations have greatly reduced the incidents of this type of injury.

- Don't put scarves, necklaces, or cords of any kind in the playpen or crib. Entanglement can occur, and that could cause strangulation. Ribbons around the necks of stuffed toys may tragically find their way around a child's neck or cause choking. Remove them altogether.

- Make sure that you have a safe toy box. Ensure it has a lid support that prevents it from accidentally slamming down. Serious head injuries have resulted from slamming lids. Strangulation has also been caused by a toy box when a child's neck has been squeezed by a lid that is too heavy.

B. Window Blind Cords

In September 1992, the Product Safety Bureau, Health Canada issued a warning bulletin to parents and caregivers about the

Children Can Strangle on Blind and Curtain Cords

DANGER!

danger of strangulation that could arise if young children became tangled in the pull cords for window blinds or drapes. In Canada, in the three-year period between 1989 and 1992, there were seven deaths due to strangulation from cords. There were also twelve near-fatalities reported between 1986 and 1990. In the U.S.A. there have been seventy-six deaths reported since 1981. The majority of the children involved in these events were under three years of age.

The following tips make the installation and use of window blinds safer around young children:

Cord Shorteners

- When purchasing new blinds or drapes, ask for short cords. If the blinds or drapes come with long cords, tie or hang the cord near the top of the window.

- Make sure young children will not be able to reach window cords or chains. Keep dangling cords from blinds and curtains away from cribs, playpens, or other child equipment.

- Some people cut the loop part of the blind cords into two pieces. While this practice will help reduce the chance of strangulation, there will still be two pieces of cord within the reach of the child, increasing the potential for danger. Again, make sure the children cannot reach the cords.

You can secure the cords using one of several methods:

- Clip the cord to itself or to the window blind with a clamping device such as a clothes pin or a cord clip.

- Wrap or tie the cord to itself.

- Wrap the cord around a cleat securely mounted near the top of the window blind.

- Install a tie down device in the floor or the window sill when a long cord is necessary.

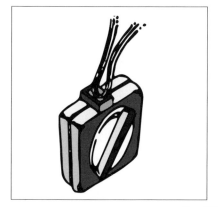 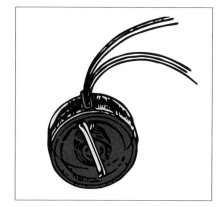

Cord Shorteners

Choking, Suffocation, Strangulation, and Drowning   23

C. Ropes on the Playground and Drawstrings on Clothing

Playgrounds pose special dangers for strangulation incidents. Children have strangled when they have become entangled in ropes or skipping ropes attached to playground equipment. Similarly, the cords and drawstrings on coats or sweatshirts worn by children have been blamed in the strangulation deaths of children when the cords were snagged in playground equipment. Again, these events can take place in the blink of an eye. Never leave young children unsupervised on a playground. By the end of 1995 in the U.S.A., most clothing manufactures will have eliminated drawstrings from children's clothing.

- Inspect the playground before your child uses it. Constant supervision of young children on a playground is essential. Should a strangulation occur, you will be able to respond quickly; hopefully, you can prevent a fatality.

- Always remove ropes tied to trees or to playground equipment such as slides and climbing apparatus.

- Always shorten, tie up, or even completely remove cords and drawstrings on all articles of your child's clothing. These cords are mostly decorative and serve little purpose. Fasten chin straps on caps and bonnets.

2. Suffocation

Suffocation is a common cause of death among infants, toddlers, and young children. Suffocation can happen very easily and it can occur in a wide variety of situations. Deaths have resulted when children put plastic bags over their head, or when they have become tangled up in dry-cleaning bags. Suffocation has resulted when a crib support broke and a child was wedged between the mattress and side support. Children have suffocated when they were placed on waterbeds, and everything from toy boxes to snow tunnels are potential suffocation hazards. Keep in mind the following tips to help prevent suffocation.

In a controlled test situation a six week-old child was placed on a water bed and video taped. The tape showed the infant falling asleep face down. Her face including the nose and mouth, remained trapped and relatively immobile in the depression (Hazards of Mattresses, Beds and Bedding in Deaths of Infants. The American Journal of Forensic Medicine and Pathology 12(1): 27-32, 1991).

- Keep any type of plastic, nylon, or cloth bags away from children. Deaths have resulted when children have pulled dry-cleaning bags from hanging clothes stored in closets. Children have suffocated when they put the bags over their head and then could not remove them. This kind of situation can happen surprisingly fast. There are warnings on the bags about suffocation; they are there for a reason. Do not leave bags lying around your house. Tie them into knots and dispose of them immediately.

- Keep plastic garbage bags out of the reach of children. Remember to safely store the bags that you keep in the garage for yard work.

- Young children have died of suffocation in unsafe play-pens when their head became trapped between two of the plastic layers of the playpen's floor padding.

- If you live in an area that gets snow, and you have a steep roof, do not let your children play under the eaves. Snow may slide off the roof and bury a child. If you need to shovel snow off your roof, keep the children indoors and out of the way. When shoveled snow hits the ground, it lands with a surprising amount of force, enough to break a child's neck.

- If your children are making snow tunnels, make sure the tunnels are sound and cannot collapse on them.

- There have been many suffocation deaths involving waterbeds. In most instances the child was lying face down. Infants should sleep on a firm, flat surface.

- The head of an infant can be buried in the deep folds of fluffy bed clothes or rugs. The bedding covers a child's mouth and nose; some children may even die from suffocation in this manner. Do not use soft fluffy materials under an infant.

- Bead-filled cushions, especially those that resemble a large bean bag, present a real danger to infants. A suffocation hazard arises if a child is placed face down on these cushions. The weight of an infant's head causes an indentation in the cushion's surface and the child may not be able to lift her head high enough to breathe freely.

- "Overlying deaths" happen when an infant or child is pinned beneath another person and suffocation results. In some cases, an unconscious or sleeping parent, or a sibling caused the situation. Careless alcohol consumption and/or the use of other drugs while caring for a child can increase the chance of this happening.

3. Choking

Eating is one of the activities we take for granted: we usually do not think that eating can be dangerous. However, many children and adults die every year from choking on food. A child's airway is approximately the diameter of his little finger, so it is easy to see that ingesting solid foods and the inadvertent ingesting of objects poses a very high danger. I have listed a few of the more dangerous foods for small children and included a warning about objects children frequently swallow. Here are some important steps that you can take to prevent a choking tragedy.

Take a recognized CPR from a professional agency that meets the guidelines of the Heart and Stroke Foundation of Canada. You will learn methods to deal with the choking child. For example, in these classes you will learn how to use the invaluable "Heimlich Manoeuvre" to assist a choking adult and child. You will also learn that this manoeuvre is different from the technique you should use to help an infant.

In 1986, an eight year-old boy was eating a hot dog when the wiener became lodged in his airway. People on the scene and the ambulance attendants tried the recommended procedures to remove it. When they arrived at the hospital, the staff with additional equipment were able to remove it, but unfortunately, it was too late to save the child's life.

- Wieners can be dangerous. Many children have died when a piece of wiener has blocked the airway. If you do feed wieners to children, cut them lengthwise and into small pieces.

- Peanuts are the perfect size to block a small air passage. Grapes, peas, beans, and hard candies are some other common foods that may block an airway. Either avoid feeding these foods to small children altogether, or else cut up, crush, or mash the food before serving it.

- Teach your children good eating habits. This means that they should not talk, laugh, fight, or yell with food in their mouth.

- Do not let your children run with food in their mouths. It is all too common for parents to give their child food in an outdoor social setting and then tell her to run and play with her friends.

- Keep all pet food away from children; choking may result from hard or soft pet foods. Children are naturally curious about how pet food tastes. Teach your child that his pet's food is not people food and that it does not taste like people food.

- Objects such as pennies, tacks, pen caps, and other tiny bright objects attract children and can cause choking. Do not give your children a chance to put these things into their mouth.

- Make sure buttons and decorations on stuffed animals, toys, clothing, and decorations are securely attached. Remove ribbons from stuffed animals. A baby may pull insecurely fastened decorations off toys and put them

Choking, Suffocation, Strangulation, and Drowning   27

into his mouth. Check your child's toys and clothing regularly for loose or broken parts.

- Eraser heads from pencils, the rubber ends of spring coil door stops, and countless other unlikely, though seemingly "attached" parts have been pried off, bitten off, or pulled off larger objects and then choked on. Examine your child's environment regularly to see what attracts her and what could pose a choking hazard.

- Remember that thick carpets can hide small objects that could cause a child to choke. Magnets from fridges, or pins and tacks from cork boards may fall onto the floor, and lie there waiting for little hands to put them into little mouths. Examine floor surfaces regularly from a child's eye view. Frequent vacuuming and sweeping will collect more than dust.

- Small bits of soap can become a choking hazard in a child's hands. When the soap bar gets too small, dispose of it.

Check Choking

Kids for Keeps

A. Pacifiers

Child deaths have been attributed to the use of unsafe pacifiers. The safest pacifiers are of a one-piece construction that does not have detachable parts and has a large rigid shield to prevent the pacifier from slipping too far into the baby's mouth. A pacifier should be strong enough so that it doesn't break down with constant use.

- Never put a string around a baby's neck and through the pacifier's ring.

- Inspect the pacifier often to look for signs of any deterioration. The rubber will break down with age, heat, and contact with sunlight or food. Broken pieces may be swallowed or a child may choke on them. Discard if holes or tears appear.

- The ring of a pacifier should be hinged or flexible enough to prevent the pacifier from being forced into the baby's mouth should the baby roll over onto his face.

- Pacifiers should be kept clean; wash them often.

Choking, Suffocation, Strangulation, and Drowning   29

B. Balloons

In North America alone, balloons have killed 127 children when they put them into their mouth and choked on them. Balloons can be extremely hard to remove from the airway with standard first aid measures, because the latex has a tendency to mould to the airway. Balloons given as promotional giveaways should not be given to small children. Older children will invariably receive balloons in a variety of situations; here are some tips to keep them safe.

- Keep children from sucking or chewing on either inflated or uninflated balloons.

- Get rid of broken balloons at once; make sure you collect all the pieces of a broken balloon.

- Adults should inflate balloons for children rather than allowing the child to do it himself.

- Keep uninflated balloons away from children.

Balloon Alert

4. Drowning

Drowning is an all-too-frequent cause of death in children and adults. Drowning tragedies can take place virtually anywhere. Children have drowned in ponds, lakes, swimming pools, wading pools, bathtubs, toilets and even buckets of water. It doesn't matter where water and young children come together, children need constant supervision around water. Many fatalities have resulted when the child was left for "just a second or two." Remember, children can drown in very shallow water; only a couple of inches is more than enough to drown a child.

In one case in 1990, I responded to a possible drowning. When I arrived, a father was holding his limp, two year-old boy in the backyard by the swimming pool. The child had been left in the backyard with older children, supposedly for only a very short time. The older children left and the parents were sidetracked in the house. The two year-old fell into the swimming pool. I cannot put into words the horror and the pain I saw in the parents' faces when we arrived. Resuscitation attempts proved to be unsuccessful.

- Never leave your child unattended in or near the bathtub, pool, wading pool, or any other body of water. Supervise children at all times when they are around water. Children have drowned even when several adults have been close by "supervising" them. In social situations make sure one adult is the designated supervisor; rotate the responsibility.

- If you have a swimming pool, make sure your children, as well as other children in the neighborhood, will not be able to get near the pool unsupervised.

- Drain wading pools after use.

- Phone calls should never take priority over the supervision of a child in water. A cordless phone can make things easier for you when you are bathing the child or are around the pool; you won't have to take the children with you to answer the phone. Never let a telephone call distract your attention from supervision.

- Empty all buckets of water around the house and yard. Children have fallen head first into cleaning buckets without tipping the bucket over, and drowned. Surprisingly, this kind of problem is fairly common. Some bucket manufacturers now include a warning about a possible child drowning hazard in their labeling.

- Infants have drowned in pet food bowls when their faces were submerged in the bowl and the child's weak neck muscles were not able to lift their face out of the water.

- Keep toilet lids down. It is a good idea to install a locking system that will keep the lid closed and make opening difficult for a child.

Water Watch

- Barrels to catch rain water should have child-proof lids. A curious child will want to see what's inside.
- Fence off waterholes, ponds, and dugouts to keep children out.
- Septic tanks, wells, and other hazards should be covered to prevent children from falling into them. The covers should be designed so that it is impossible for a child or even several children acting together to open them. A sheet of plywood covering a water-filled hole is insufficient to keep children out.

Poisoning

4

P oisons, according to the Poison Control Center, are any substance considered to be harmful. Poisons can be swallowed, splashed into the eyes, spilled on the skin, or breathed in. Medication becomes poison when it is taken by the wrong person, or in the wrong amount.

Babies between the ages of seven to twelve months move around a good deal, and they seem to get into everything. At this age they can pull objects down from tables and shelves that they were not able to reach earlier; and they tend to put everything into their mouth. It is easy for them to reach products stored in areas such as cupboards under sinks and coffee tables. Plants are also a common problem for children because they tend to experiment by chewing on them.

Household products poison many children every year. When children are between one and three years old they can really get into things. They explore by putting objects in their mouth. Their taste sense is not well developed, so they will drink or eat seemingly distasteful substances. They are very curious, very mobile, and they can reach things that are stored above their eye level. Remember, too, that children between three and five years old will imitate behavior. If you put things into your mouth they will want to do so, too.

There are countless ways children get into drugs and chemicals. The scenarios for trouble are almost endless. Events in a normal adult's environment may be catastrophic for a young child. For instance, many people keep vitamins and prescription pills on the kitchen table so they will not forget to take them. These become handy for a toddler, mimicking his parent, to "take" them also. Some other potentially disastrous circum-

> *Once while flying in a plane, I read a short story about a certain brand of crayons with a high lead content that was available in the United States. Next to me, my child was playing with some crayons that the flight attendant had given us. They were the same type that the article described. The airlines no longer use this brand of crayons.*

stances are these: baby has wet hands and puts his fingers into the dishwasher detergent and rubs his eyes; baby chews on a plant when you are visiting friends and she begins to go into convulsions; baby decides to try your mouthwash. It is to be expected that children might want to get into the alcohol cabinet, but did you know that a mouthful of some mouthwashes also has enough alcohol to cause problems? We do not tend to think of alcohol as being a poison, but it can be deadly.

We must try to anticipate every possible situation where a child can get into chemicals, medicines, alcohol, or any other substance that might cause your child harm. Parents and caregivers have to concern themselves not only about their own medications, but also the medications belonging to visitors in the child's home. It is far too common for children to overdose on medication from someone who is just visiting. We must be extremely careful and attuned to the changing environment of our children; every day a hazard to them might escape our notice.

Many poisonings have happened at the home of grandparents. For example, grandpa's bottle of denture cleaner falls from the cabinet onto the floor and baby gets into it. Or a child is placed in grandmother's bed for a nap, and grandmother happens to keep her heart pills on the night table. Even though grandparents, obviously, have raised their own children, they may have forgotten how quickly children can get into trouble. Their normal routine may be to leave their medication on the kitchen table and forget about the danger when the grandchildren are visiting.

Deadly Diet

Poisonings are the fourth most common cause of death among Canadian children. The majority of poisonings occur in those younger than 5 years at home and involve medicines. Personal care products, plants and household cleaners are also common poisons.

Learn about the poison control center in you area. Check the phone book for the number in your area and keep the number close to your phone. Poison proof your home. Know what substances are poisonous and their locations. Here are some poison hazards you can prevent:

1. Baby Products and Personal Care Products

- Keep all baby care products in a safe place. Surprisingly, many baby care products found in the nursery can make your child sick. For example, many medications for navel cord care contain alcohol, and ingesting even very small amounts can be dangerous for an infant.

- Baby creams and oils should be kept away from your child. If your child ingests them, vomiting and diarrhea can result. These substances can also be aspirated into your child's lungs, where they can cause more serious problems.

- Keep all medications out of reach of your children at all times. Medicine cabinets and storage cabinets for household cleaners should be kept locked and off-limits at all times. Return hazardous items to safe storage immediately after use.

- When you are giving your child medications, read the directions carefully. Do not administer medicine in the dark. It is too easy to make a mistake.

- Never call medications candy. Children will not learn to distinguish pills they may find around the house from "candy."

- Do not take medications in front of your child. Little eyes may be watching and a child could imitate you.

- Keep the medications in the original container. The lid should be child resistant. And remember that just because pill bottles are child resistant does not mean they are child-proof. Poisonings have happened when parents did not properly replace the lids on child-resistant containers.

- Get rid of old medications that you will not be using. Most drug stores will dispose of them safely for you.

- Store products in original containers. Pour solutions carefully so that labels stay dry and readable.

- Personal care products, perfumes, and even cosmetics can be a serious poisoning risk. For example, many mouthwashes and skin products contain alcohol. It takes very little alcohol to put a child into an alcohol coma.

- If you have company visiting, make sure your child will not get into their luggage, toiletries, and medications.

- When you travel, keep track of the toiletries and medications in your luggage. Remember that many poisonings happen in the home of grandparents.

- Purchase products with childproof packaging.

2. Chemicals in the Home, Yard, and Garage

- When using a substance such as furniture polish, cleanser, or any other kind of chemical, make sure you put it away immediately when you are finished with it, and before you do anything else. Keep detergent and bleach out of children's reach. Many poisonings occur when the child is left alone for just a few seconds.

- Never put products such as gasoline, oil, or turpentine in pop bottles. Children may think it is pop and drink it.

- Use safety latches to help keep chemicals and other substances away from children. However, never put all of your trust in safety latches; they are not 100% child-proof.

- Even empty containers may have enough residue of the original substance to poison your child. Remember, little bodies do not need to ingest nearly as much of a poisonous substance as you would, to become very sick.

- Keep batteries away from children. The small button-like batteries that are found in calculators and watches have been, on occasion, swallowed or choked on by children. The acid from inside other batteries is potentially dangerous. Young children have enough energy; they don't need the extra power. Seriously, remember that these batteries could kill.

- Do not keep chemicals such as drain cleaners under the sink in the kitchen or bathrooms. Keep them out of reach or in a locked cupboard.

- Remember to keep the chemicals in your yard and garage out of reach. All too frequently children in the back yard with mom and dad get into toxic substances when their parents are distracted for only a second.

- Use extreme caution if you are using fertilizers, or pest or weed killers. Grass or plants will still have toxins on their foliage hours after the application of pesticides. Insect or animal poisons may be moved from where you put them to another location. Store these products safely, and when you do use them, read and follow the manufacturer's directions.

- Open doors and windows before using products that have fumes.

A family went to visit friends who lived on a farm. While the adults visited, the children, two and five years of age, played behind the couch in the family room. The two year-old boy suddenly fell to the floor, unconscious. The child appeared to have had a seizure. A small grain of oat or barley was found in his mouth. Searching the house, the adults found mouse poison behind the couch. Grains of the poison were piled in a crack of the family room baseboard; originally the poison had been placed in the basement, and presumably it was moved by a mouse. The five year-old said that her brother was playing with the grain and ate several pieces of it. The boy collapsed about ten minutes after ingesting the poison. The child was in a coma for three days; fortunately, he was discharged after a two-week stay in the hospital.

---

3. Plants

Plants are found in most homes and in just about every yard. What many people fail to realize is that many of the plants and shrubs that adults take for granted are poisonous — especially to children. Ingesting even small portions of some of the plants found around the house can cause reactions ranging from mild distress to serious complications, such as having airway swelling and closure or having a complete kidney shutdown. The result could be the death of a child.

The first step toward the prevention of this kind of poisoning is to be able to recognize the type of plants you have. If you are not sure whether the plants you have are poisonous, you can check with a local florist, nursery, or your local poison control center.

The seriousness of plant poisoning depends upon the amount swallowed. Ingesting even a small amount of some plants can be dangerous. People may be harmed in several ways: there may be irritation of the stomach and intestines; there may be poisoning of the system; there may be mouth and throat lining irritation; and/or there may be skin irritation. The seriousness of the poisoning usually depends upon the amount of the toxin with which the person has come into contact. If you suspect plant poisoning, call the Poison Control Center immediately. Some poisonous plants are listed below.

Azalea	Honeysuckle
Baneberry	Hyacinth
Bird of Paradise	Hydrangea
Bittersweet	Jerusalem Cherry
Black Locust	Laburnum
Buckthorn	Lily-of-the-Valley
Caladium	Mayapple
Calla Lilly	Mistletoe
Castor Bean	Narcissus
Cyclamen	Nightshades
Daffodil	Oleander
Daphne	Philodendron
Dieffenbachia	Privet
Elephant's Ear	Sedum
English Ivy	Tulip
Foxglove	Wild Parsnip
Hawthorn	Yew
Holly	

4. Lead Poisoning

We have known for a long time that lead is hazardous to our health. We now realize that even small amounts can be dangerous. Infants and children are especially vulnerable to lead because they absorb it more easily than adults. In addition, lead absorbed by an expectant mother can harm the unborn child. The amount of lead taken into the body depends on the amount of lead we are exposed to and for how long. Prolonged exposure to small amounts can cause poisoning that is as serious as short exposure to large amounts.

The signs and symptoms of lead poisoning are often similar to other childhood complaints. Symptoms include headaches, irritability, tiredness, lack of appetite, and stomach aches. Because these symptoms are similar to other complaints, a physician may not suspect lead poisoning. Examine your child's environment for potential sources of lead.

Lead used to be an ingredient in paint that was used to help it dry faster, wear better, and to make the colors more vibrant. Paint manufacturers in Canada decreased the use of lead in their products between 1950 and 1976. And in 1976, The Hazardous Product Act limited the amount of lead that could be used in paints. Children living in older homes are at risk where lead based paint has been used. Chipped or peeling paint increases the hazard; these unstable surfaces can be chewed on or the chips can be ingested. Contaminated dust is a serious risk for babies and children. Not only can they be poisoned by breathing in the dust, but they can absorb a significant amount of lead by putting things which are covered in contaminated dust into their mouths.

Be cautious of old hand-me-down wooden toys because lead-based paints may have been used to decorate them. When lead paint is sanded or removed with heat, the dust and paint chips can be very toxic. Check with your local health board for tips on removing the paint safely.

Lead can also be found in tap water if solder with a high lead content was used when the plumbing was installed. At the turn of the twentieth century, many household pipes had a high lead content. Another possible source of lead is some pottery. If you are not sure that your pottery is lead free you should refrain from using it.

Owners of homes built after 1980 should not be concerned about lead levels in interior paints. However, if you suspect lead poisoning in the house, a professional lab will be able to test samples. *(Home Renovations - Removing Lead-Based Paints, Health Protection Branch of Health and Welfare Canada, February, 1992)*

Allergic Reactions 5

Peple are allergic to many different substances. Allergies are hypersensitive or pathological reactions to environmental factors or substances that usually do not affect most people. Some of the more common things people are allergic to are the following: pollens, dust, insect bites, peanuts, shellfish, and certain plants. To some people, coming into contact with these substances can mean death from a condition called **anaphylaxis**. Anaphylaxis is a hypersensitivity of tissues in the body to what the body considers a foreign substance. These reactions range from mild to intense. An allergic reaction may evolve within hours, but some are almost instantaneous. Serious allergic reactions too often can result in the death of a child.

If you suspect your child is allergic to something, seek medical aid immediately. Talk to your physician; there are certain medications you can obtain to help relieve this condition. Remember, even after you have administered the medication, medical aid should be sought.

Allergic reactions can potentially be a life-threatening condition. If you suspect an allergic reaction, and the symptoms are severe, call an ambulance immediately.

Some of the common signs and symptoms of an allergic reaction are these:

- Profuse sweat, flushed face, or red blotches on the skin.

- Hives — which are raised, reddened areas on the skin.

- Wheezing — the child may have difficulty breathing, and may begin to make wheezing noises.

- Labored breathing — the child has to work hard to breathe.

- Abdominal pain — accompanied by stomach cramps, diarrhea, and/or vomiting.

- Numbness of the mouth or limbs.

Protect your child from allergic reactions by taking these preventative steps:

- When you suspect your child has allergies, begin recording the suspected causes and consult your pediatrician immediately.

- Have your child tested for allergies. Test results may take some time, but it is worth going through the procedures to determine the problem substances and the correct treatment.

- Follow your physician's instructions for treating the allergy. Medication and avoidance are the two most common types of treatment; others include techniques for the gradual desensitization to the allergen. Frequently, people "grow out of" allergies; however, some people develop them at different stages of life, effectively "growing into" them.

- Alert all caregivers, teachers, and baby-sitters about your child's allergies, both verbally and in writing. Make sure you also inform the parents of your child's friends and your own relatives. It is important for all of these people to know of potential hazards, because any one of them may care for your child in your absence.

Burns and Scalds   **6**

B urns are the third-ranked cause of injury related deaths in Canada. In the five year period from 1987 to 1992 there were 753 children hospitalized in one province alone due to burns and scalds.

There are countless ways in which children can get burned. Playing with matches, lighters, and electrical cords often results in severe burns, or even fatalities. Children have been scalded from pulling pots of hot food from the stove onto themselves, or from exposure to extremely hot water in the bathtub. And as we all know, hot liquids burn like fire. The potential sources of burns and scalds seem almost endless. We have to teach our children from a very early age to respect the dangers of fire, electricity, and excessively hot liquids. We also have to protect them by preventing them from being exposed to situations where they might potentially get burned.

The majority of fire related deaths (more than 75%) occur in private residences. A large percentage of burned children survive, although many require long term treatment. Functional losses as well as pain and psychological problems are inestimable (Annals of Emergency Medicine Feb. 1993).

---

1. Burn Prevention in the Kitchen

- Keep handles of pots and pans turned inward, and well away from the front edge of the stove. Pots might get pulled off the stove by little ones. Cooking on the back burners may help prevent this.

- Always plan ahead before you move a hot pot, pan, or dish. Train yourself to determine where your child is in relation to you and your planned movement. Get into the habit of announcing a warning such as, "Hot stuff coming through!" Then always wait until the path is clear.

- When you are carrying hot pots and pans, use pot holders. Never handle hot pots or kettles with wet or greasy hands. You do not want to risk dropping hot food or liquids onto a child. Take precautions even if the child is several feet away from you. Hot liquids can cover a large area if they get spilled; not only will your own legs and feet get splashed, but your child may get splashed as well.

- Mop up spills promptly.

- Avoid holding your child while you are cooking at the stove or microwave. Steam and splattering fat can cause serious burns. Be especially cautious when opening microwaved packages or covered dishes; the burst of steam can burn.

- Coming into the kitchen in a rush to answer the phone or to attend to an emergency? Never sit your baby on the stove, even if you check the burners beforehand; your child might turn an element on when you're not looking.

- Install childproof knobs on the stove and use stove guards when small children are around the kitchen. Keep children far away from the stove. Remember that guards and knobs are only aids to safety; never rely on them totally.

- Keep dangling cords from hot water kettles and other electrical appliances away from the counter where they can be pulled down. The risk of things being pulled down is, of course, increased if a child is in a baby walker.

- Keep a fire extinguisher in a handy place in the kitchen. Learn how and when to use it. Consult your local fire department about the rules for identifying and extinguishing kitchen fires.

2. Preventing Scalds

- Don't hold your child while you're drinking something hot; scalds are commonly caused by spilled hot liquids. Remember that sturdy, wide-bottomed mugs may take more jostling around than more "elegant" cups before they spill the hot contents.

- Keep hot liquids — coffee, tea, grease, soup — off counters and away from young children. Be sure that appliance cords for kettles, bottle warmers, mug warmers, frying pans, and deep fat cookers are not within reach of little hands.

- Cook on the back burners and turn pot handles toward the back of the stove.

- Pre-set your hot water heater to 120F (48C) or less. Severe burns have resulted from the tap being turned on unintentionally. Consider installing a anti-scald device on the tap.

Prevention of tap water burns requires reduction in the temperature of tap water to 120F (48C). At this temperature, it takes 10 minutes of exposure to cause full thickness burns in adult skin; at 125F (52C), the corresponding time is 2 minutes; at 130F (54C) the time is 30 seconds. Exposure to a water temperature of 140F (60C) for only three seconds can result in third degree burns that would require hospitalization and skin grafts.

Out of Harm's Way

Scalds happen frequently to young children at home but can be prevented. One to two seconds exposure to 65°C (150°F) hot water will result in a serious burn. The most common scald in the home is caused by spilled coffee, tea or other hot drinks.

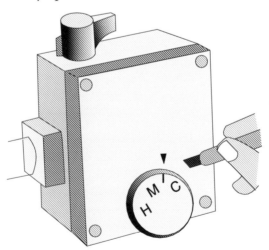

Hot Water Tank Gauge
Keep Water Temperature at 48°C (120°F) or lower

- Test the water before you put your child into the bath.

- Never leave infants or young children unsupervised in the bathtub — not even to answer the phone. Don't let older children prepare baths for youngsters unless you are absolutely sure that they will consciously keep the water temperature low and will be able to conduct themselves appropriately in case of an emergency.

3. Safety and Electricity

- Cover all electrical outlets that are not being used with safety plugs or childproof electrical outlet covers. When you use an outlet, remember to replace the safety plug immediately after you finish using it.

- Do not leave light bulb sockets empty when a lamp is plugged in; little fingers may find their way into them. Use socket safety plugs.These will help reduce the chance of your children sticking an object into the socket.

- Keep electrical cords out of your baby's reach. Use cord shorteners, or tape electrical cords to the walls or under furniture. Remember that children have been known to bite electrical cords. The devastating result can be severe burns to the mouth that may disfigure or even kill. Of course, electrocution is also a possibility.

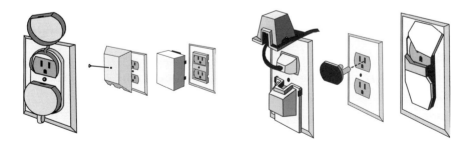

Safety Plugs

- Don't forget that there are electrical plugs on the outside of your house and in your garage. Take appropriate precautions.

- Do not leave appliances such as hair dryers, vacuum cleaners, and irons plugged in when they are not in use.

4. Fire Safety

In Canada there are approximately four hundred fire deaths related to home fires every year. Children account for many of those fatalities. Smoke detectors and a plan for what to do in case of a fire might have prevented many of these deaths.

Real fires do not act like the ones that you see in the movies. A residential fire is usually characterized by intense heat and black heavy smoke that makes it very difficult to see, and especially to breathe. In fact, in most residential fires, the cause of death is not the flames themselves, but smoke inhalation. In most cases, it is not the flames of a fire that will reach you first, but the smoke and the extreme heat. When materials burn, they release many poisonous substances that are carried in the smoke. People have died of smoke inhalation in their sleep, never having wakened to the flames outside the bedroom door.

Close to 90 percent of residential fire deaths occurred in homes without smoke alarms or where smoke alarms were not functioning. Far too frequently, people remove batteries from smoke alarms to use for other reasons. Remarkably, some people remove them to stop the annoyance from the beeping that signals a low battery in the unit.

House fires that involve children are especially devastating. Children under five are the people who are at greatest risk during fires. Often they hide in closets or under beds. They may need special help to escape. Every family should have a fire evacuation plan.

The speed at which fire can spread is unbelievable. Many people try to put out large fires themselves; this is very dangerous.

Another mistake people make is that once they are safely out of the house that is on fire, they run back in to retrieve a pet, a wallet, or a family heirloom. That last run is often a fatal mistake. Once you are out of a burning building, **do not go back in**. You will not survive in the heavy smoke and intense heat. Leave the job to fire fighting professionals with appropriate equipment. Their chances of success are far greater than yours.

Here are some fire prevention tips for your home:

- Never leave matches or lighters lying around the house. Children will find them and the results can be devastating. Make sure visitors do not leave their lighters lying around. Never use your lighter as a toy or a soother for the child.

Lighting Up

Burns and Scalds

- Teach your children that if they find matches or lighters, they should give them to adults. Praise them when they do so.

- Be careful if you are a smoker! The majority of fire related fatalities are caused by careless smoking. Check the sofa for any cigarettes or ashes that might have fallen between the cushions. Wet your ash trays before going to bed or leaving the house. Do not dump ashtrays into the garbage. Never smoke in bed.

- Keep your child away from the fireplace or wood stove. There have been incidents where children have fallen into a fireplace. Guards can be purchased that will help stop your child from getting too close to the fireplace or wood stove.

- Keep a screen or glass doors around the fireplace to help keep children from getting too close and to keep sparks away from them and their clothing.

- Make sure the areas around furnaces, fireplaces, and wood stoves are clear of combustible materials such as magazines and newspapers.

- Keep hallways and exits clear of toys and other objects.

5. Smoke Alarms

Many home fires happen in the night when people are asleep. Smoke alarms should be placed outside each sleeping area. You should also have one on every floor of the house. Test them regularly and when a low battery signal comes to your attention, replace the battery promptly.

There are two main types of alarms: photoelectric and ionization. Either is suitable for home fire prevention. Make sure the alarms have Underwriters Laboratories (UL) or Canadian Standards Association (CSA) labels. Smoke alarms can be powered by batteries or wired to the house power. It is a good idea to have both types, so that one system can back up the other.

- Be sure everyone is familiar with the sound of the smoke detector and understands that it means to get out NOW!

- Battery operated systems will usually beep on a regular basis when the battery is low. The batteries should be changed immediately. Do not take a battery out without replacing it. They should be changed at least once a year; pick a date such as New Year's Day or someone's birthday and remember to do it every year.

- Test the smoke alarm by allowing the smoke from a freshly extinguished candle to drift up to it. This test should be done at least once a month. Some models have a test button that you press to sound the alarm. Note that this test, while useful for testing the alarm itself, does not test the smoke sensing system.

- Clean the detectors on a regular basis; dust buildup can cause false alarms or malfunctions. Follow manufacturers' directions for cleaning.

- If you have been away for a few days, check the detectors when you return.

6. Escape Plan

Once you have been alerted to a fire you must escape. Have an escape plan in order. Draw up a plan of your house and mark escape routes from anywhere in the house. Each room should have a primary and an alternate escape route. You should have a pre-arranged meeting place where everyone can go as soon as they are out of the house. This could be a tree, a street light, or a neighbor's front door. Make sure the meeting place is a safe distance from the house. Your escape plan should be practiced on a regular basis. Have someone sound the alarm and do a rehearsal of what you would do and where you would escape to in case of a fire.

Review the plan frequently with all the members of the family. Ask your local fire department for more information about fire prevention.

Teach your children that in case of a fire they must not hide in closets or under the bed. Hiding makes it much harder for a firefighter to locate them when they are doing a search of the house. Explain to them that if they see a firefighter during a fire he will be wearing a mask and look scary; they should run to him and not away.

Once you are out of the house, make sure everybody is accounted for and do not go back to the site until the fire department tells you it is safe to do so.

If there is a fire in your home, here are the proper responses:

- Get out of bed and crawl to the door. Smoke and heat rise; it is therefore both easier to breath and cooler at lower levels.

- Touch the door; if it is hot, do not open it. If the door is cool to the touch, still open the door very slowly, because there may be intense heat on the other side. If the hallway is full of smoke or fire is visible, close the door and use an alternate exit.

- When exiting, stay low and close doors behind you. Closed doors will help slow the spread of the fire.

- Get out of the house and stay out.

- Phone the fire department from a neighbor's house.

- If your clothes catch on fire do not run or stand, but Stop, Drop and Roll immediately. Drop to the ground and cover your face with your hands and roll over and over. Practice this maneuver with your children. Explain to them that rolling smothers the flames.

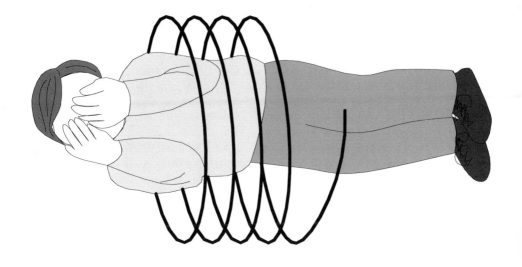

Stop Drop and Roll

7. Clothing and Fire

Many countries have standards on children's clothing which manufacturers have to meet. For example, since 1987 in Canada, it should no longer be possible for you to buy a child's cotton nightgown. A nightgown can be especially dangerous because it is easy for the flowing material to brush up against sources of ignition. Once the nightgown is on fire, the gown acts like a chimney and flames can race up the gown very quickly.

The National Fire Protection Association recommends that you avoid loose, fuzzy, lightweight clothing because of a high risk of flammability. Instead, the child's clothing should be a sturdy, tightly woven fabric that does not fit too loosely.

8. Camping and Fire Safety

Campfire burns accounted for 68% of recreational burns treated at Alberta firefighters' burn units. Be extremely careful with your children when you are camping. It is very easy for a child to fall into a campfire. Remember, too, children (like adults) are often mesmerized by the open flames and will want to "play" with the fire by poking it with a stick or adding fuel to the flames. Teach your children to respect fire. Your lessons will be strengthened by your own example.

- Never leave children unsupervised around a campfire, even for a second. Ensure a proper adult/child ratio when groups gather around a campfire.

- Make a rule that bans horseplay close to a fire pit.

- When building a campfire, do not use gasoline as a starter. The flash flame from igniting fuel-soaked materials can reach several feet beyond the perimeters of the fire pit and severely injure bystanders.

- Build a fire suitable to the task at hand, and avoid huge bonfires when children are present. Always be alert to changing wind conditions and watch for flying sparks and embers. Keep away from the down wind side of a fire.

- In addition to flash and flame burns, children are at risk for severe contact burns, particularly at campfires built in sand pits. Because ringed pits resemble sandboxes, many children mistake them for play equipment.

- Children need to be taught that the stones ringing a fire pit become extremely hot and can not only burn little hands, but can melt the bottoms of shoes. Be alert to hot coals and embers that may fly outside of the fire perimeter. This is a good reason to ban bare feet near a campfire.

- Often people extinguish pit fires by smothering them with sand. Unfortunately, this practice can create an oven in which coals continue to burn for hours. Children have sustained third degree burns that have required skin grafts after contact with the hot sand. Extinguish pit fires by dousing them with water, stirring the ashes, and pouring more water over the site. Repeat this procedure until the pit is completely extinguished

- Most tents are very flammable. Fatalities have occurred when tents in which children were sleeping caught fire. Make sure children do not have matches or a lighter when they are "camping out."

- When cooking on a campfire, pick up pots and pans with a pot holder — and only after you know where bystanders are, in relationship to your planned path.

- When roasting marshmallows, assist young children. Never shake a flaming marshmallow — it could turn into a flying, flaming, napalm-like ball.

The Child's Room 7

When a new baby is on the way, many new parents take great pride in decorating and furnishing the room for the new arrival. Quite often we forget, or just don't realize, the potential hazards that may lurk in the old crib that your parents gave to you, or the change table that your uncle made. Keep in mind some of the safety tips listed below.

1. The Crib

Cribs built before the Fall of 1986 do not meet Canadian safety standards. There have been deaths in older style cribs due to the result of the mattress support giving way. Mattresses were formerly supported by S-hooks. If a child bounced in the crib, or if the support was pushed up on from underneath by another child or pet it was possible for the mattress support to come off the S-hooks, resulting in the collapse of the support. In newer cribs, the mattress support is bolted in place.

- If possible, try to obtain a new crib which meets the most recent safety standards. Make sure the mattress is flat and firm and that all mattress supports are firmly in place. Test the crib by shaking, pounding on the mattress, and on the mattress support from underneath. Make sure the bolts securing the mattress supports are tight.

A family bought a second-hand crib that was described as being "in good condition" at the time of purchase. As it happened, it had been damaged during assembly. A seven month old child became trapped between a broken moveable side rail and the side of the mattress and was asphyxiated.

- Mattresses should not be more than 6 inches (15.5 cm) deep and should have a firm surface. The space between the mattress and the side of the crib should be no more than $1^3/_{16}$ inches (3 cm). Confirm this by pushing the mattress into one corner and measuring the gap between the mattress and the opposite corner.

Old Cribs Can Kill

Crib safety standards were changed in 1986 to increase safety. However, 17 deaths in Canada have occurred since then in cribs built before 1986.

- Don't keep the crib or change table under a window. A misdirected ball or rock could shower your child with glass. And remember that window blind cords pose a strangulation hazard.

- Check on the baby often to make sure she is still in her crib or playpen.

- When changing sheets or moving the crib, check the crib again for loose or damaged parts.

Babies have very weak neck muscles. This means they are unable to lift their head when they are lying on their stomach. Suffocation is a serious risk to newborns. Here are some tips for crib safety:

- Avoid using a plastic sheet on the crib mattress.

- Never let a baby sleep with a pillow.

- Never leave a bib around an infant's neck during naps.

- Don't put the baby to sleep on a waterbed. Infants have suffocated in the soft, water-filled mattress. There are also other problems with waterbeds: babies have been bounced off the bed by siblings, or been trapped between the side of the mattress and the bed frame.

- Help prevent suffocation by keeping large stuffed animals, pillows, and heavy blankets out of the crib.

- A baby's head can be hurt if it gets banged against the sides of a crib. Soft crib bumpers are a good idea to help protect your baby's head. Make sure the crib bumpers are firmly secured to the railings and that they fit snugly against the slats of the crib so that the head cannot be caught between the crib sides and the mattress.

- Make sure the ties or fasteners on the bumpers are kept short.

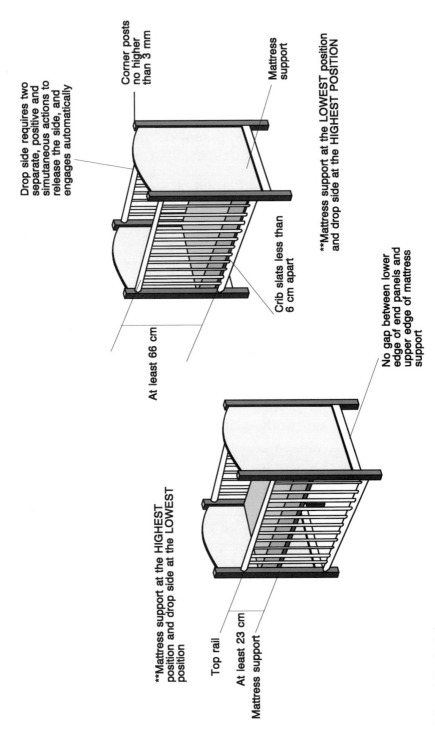

Drop side requires two separate, positive and simultaneous actions to release the side, and engages automatically

Corner posts no higher than 3 mm

Mattress support

At least 66 cm

Crib slats less than 6 cm apart

**Mattress support at the LOWEST position and drop side at the HIGHEST POSITION

**Mattress support at the HIGHEST position and drop side at the LOWEST position

Top rail

At least 23 cm

Mattress support

No gap between lower edge of end panels and upper edge of mattress support

Crib and Cradle Safety

- The crib railings should always be up and in the locked position.

- When the baby can stand up, make sure the mattress is in the lowest position and that there is nothing in the crib that the baby can stand on (such as stuffed toys or bumper pads) to enable her to crawl over the top of the railing.

To reduce the chance of strangulation in the crib:

- Never hang strings, cords, or ribbons from the crib.

- Keep your child's crib away from drapes, blind cords, and lamps.

- Never harness or tie your child to the crib.

- When the baby can sit up, remove all mobiles. If you leave them in place, the child will be able to reach them, and if they are pulled down, another strangulation and choking hazard is introduced.

- The railings should always be kept up and in a locked position to prevent the child from falling out. If the railing is not in a locked position, it could slide down on the child's body.

- When your child reaches 35 inches (87 cm) tall, she is too big for a crib.

2. The Change Table

When you are at home, a change table can make changing diapers much easier; in fact, change tables are now a standard part of nursery furnishings. But care must be taken when you are changing diapers. Many injuries have happened where a child has fallen off a change table onto the floor. As we all know, babies have a tendency to squirm and wriggle about, not just when they are being changed, but whenever they are not sleeping. Falls have also happened from kitchen tables, couches, and beds.

- The table should be sturdy and checked for loose parts on a regular basis.

- A good change table should have a strap to help secure the child to the table. Make sure the strap is done up, but do not rely solely on this strap. Always keep a hand on the child when he is on the table.

- Do not leave the child alone on the table for any reason, even to answer the phone. You might consider a cordless telephone to help remove the temptation to leave a child alone on the table.

- Place the table away from drapes, blind cords, or any other objects that could be of potential danger. Keep one side of the table against the wall.

- Make sure all parts of the table are in good repair. Tears in the vinyl padding of a change table can cause scrapes to a baby's delicate skin. Torn pieces of vinyl may be pulled free and put into little mouths.

- Objects such as cans of baby powder and containers of diapers should not be stored on shelves over the table because it is too easy to drop them on the baby. Most change tables have a shelf underneath the changing platform for storage of these articles.

- Make sure these objects are not left on the change table.

3. The Diaper Pail

There have been fatalities when small children have fallen head first into a diaper pail and drowned. Diaper pails should have a lock on the lid to prevent a toddler from opening the cover.

Another possible danger is the potentially poisonous deodorants used in diaper pails. The deodorant should not be accessible to the child. Many people put bleach in their diaper pails; this can be dangerous if a child inhales the bleach fumes. Serious eye damage can also result if a child splashes the bleach. Once your toddler becomes mobile the diaper pail should be stored in an area which is off limits to him.

4. The Playpen

Playpens can be an asset to a busy parent. The child is confined to a relatively small space without being isolated from the rest of the home or garden activity. Playpens are designed to be a mini-environment that will keep a child safe and content while freeing a caregiver to work nearby. However, there are some potential hazards in using playpens. Here are a few tips to make sure your baby's playpen is safe.

- Never leave a child alone or unsupervised in a playpen. Keep the playpen in sight at all times.

- Make sure the playpen meets current safety standards. Health Protection Branch, Product Safety Bureau of Health Canada introduced regulations in 1976 to help reduce playpen injuries.

- The playpen should be assembled properly each time it is set up. Follow the manufacturer's instructions. Make sure all parts that lock into place are locked and that they will not collapse. Make sure all sides are up when the child is in the playpen.

- The mattress or floor padding should be designed so that the child is unable to lift it up and get trapped between the floor and the padding. Do not add a second mattress because the infant or toddler could find herself trapped between the two.

- To reduce the chance of strangulation, do not place the playpen close to drapes, drapery cords, blinds, etc. Also keep the playpen away from electrical outlets, fire places, fans, or anything else that could be a danger.

- Clothes, diapers, or blankets left hanging on the side of the playpen could be pulled into the pen by the baby, and pose a suffocation hazard.

- Don't string toys across the playpen because a child could possibly get tangled up in the strings. If a child can reach toys on a string, there is a danger.

- Check for loose parts, or tears in the mattress or vinyl siding. Small pieces of vinyl may be torn off, partially ingested, and can potentially cause choking.

- To reduce a playpen from moving too much, it should have no more than two wheels.

- If you have a playpen with mesh sides, check for tears or cuts which could allow heads, feet, or hands to get caught. Fatalities have been caused from strangulation in older style mesh playpens when buttons on a child's clothes were caught in one of the holes of the mesh. When a child falls down, the snagged clothes can tighten around his neck. Strangulation may result.

- Once your baby is able to stand, large stuffed animals or other toys can be used as stepping stones by the child to assist in an escape.

- When your child is large enough to get out of the playpen, it no longer serves its purpose.

5. Baby Strollers

Technically, baby strollers are used more outdoors than in the child's room. But because it is a common piece of equipment associated with the early childhood years, I have included it here along with playpens.

A baby stroller is used in all types of weather and in all types of conditions. Strollers are thrown into the trunks of motor vehicles, dropped, and dragged over concrete. They carry loads they were never designed to carry. With all this wear and tear, regular safety inspections are important. There are many types and designs of strollers on the market. When choosing one, your child's safety should be your main consideration. A few things you should observe when choosing a stroller are:

- Make sure the stroller comes with the manufacturer's directions and follow them carefully.

- Choose a stroller that matches the size and age of the child who will use it.

- Never leave a child unattended in a stroller — not even for a minute!

- The stroller should be stable. If shopping bags or diaper bags are hung from the handle, the stroller's stability will be affected greatly.

- Make sure the stroller has proper restraining straps and that you use them. Injuries can happen if a child stands up and falls out of the stroller.

- The stroller should have a reliable locking mechanism to prevent unintentional folding. Make sure the brakes are in good working order.

- Don't let older siblings push the stroller with younger children in it unless they are mature enough to understand the dangers. Always supervise these situations.

6. Youth Beds and Bunk Beds

The Health Protection Branch, Product Safety Bureau of Health Canada advised consumers that the upper bunk of bunk beds may be hazardous when they are used for children under six years of age. There have been four reported deaths in Canada in the past eight years involving young children using the upper bunk (Consumer and Corporate Affairs Canada Handout, March 6, 1990).

- Children under 6 years of age should not be allowed on the top bunk.

- When purchasing a bunk bed or a toddler bed, look for consumer warnings on the product and follow them carefully. Check the bed regularly for loose or broken parts.

- When purchasing bunk beds make sure there are railings on all sides. Follow manufacturer's instructions when assembling a bunk bed or toddler bed.

- The mattress should fit snugly on all interior sides of the bed.

- The bunk bed ladder should be in good condition. Ladders are there for a purpose. Teach your children that the ladder should always be used to go up and down from the top bunk.

- Make a family rule: no jumping or bouncing on the bed!

- The wall side of the bunk bed or a toddler bed should also have a side rail. Falls between the wall and the mattress have led to suffocation or strangulation.

- Obviously there is a serious risk when a young child is on a top bunk that has no guard rails. Similarly, if guard rails are too high, the child could possibly slip between the guard rail and the mattress. This could lead to suffocation if the child's head becomes trapped and does not pass completely through the opening; his face might be forced into the mattress.

In the U.S.A., between 1985 and 1990 the Consumer Product Safety Commission received reports of over 250 infants up to twelve months of age, who suffocated on adult or youth beds. In most cases infants became wedged between the mattress and the frame or the wall. In addition, some infants suffocated while sleeping next to another sleeping person, who rolled onto the infant while still asleep. The same problems surfaced with both kinds of beds. In addition, some suffocated while in a stomach-down position in the depression of waterbeds.

- When an adult-sized twin bed is being adapted for use by a toddler, portable railings may be added to the sides. Make sure that these railings follow manufacturer's installation instructions and that they are securely attached to the sides of the bed. Examine the appropriateness of the railing: are there gaps between the top of the mattress and the railing that could entrap the head or the body of a child?

- Never leave infants on an adult or youth bed, regardless of whether the bed is a mattress-type or a waterbed. Place infants in a crib that meets federal safety standards.

- Infants can suffocate while sleeping when they become trapped between the mattress and the frame or the mattress and the wall. If an infant becomes wedged face-down on an adult or toddler mattress or sinks into a waterbed mattress, she can also suffocate.

- Choose the bed that is most appropriate for your child's stage of growth and development.

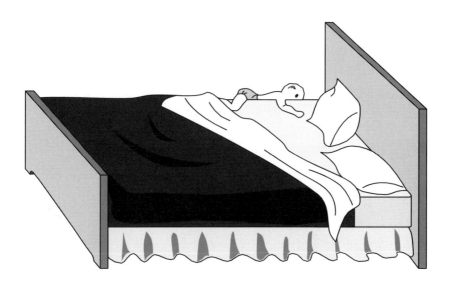

The Bathroom   8

You and your child are going to be spending quite a lot of time together in the bathroom. Giving baths, brushing teeth, washing hands, and, of course toilet training will take up many hours. This room holds many dangers such as poisonous substances, hot water, and hard, slippery surfaces. Care must be taken when in the bathroom; the bathroom is not a play area.

- Check the lock on the bathroom door to make sure you will be able to get into the bathroom after a child has locked herself in.

- Put a screw hook and eye on the bathroom door to keep the child out. Alternatively, you can purchase devices that slip onto door handles to make it more difficult to open the door. Even an old sock attached to the door knob may do the job.

- Never mix ammonia or toilet-bowl cleaner with chlorine bleach when cleaning your bathroom; the toxic gases produced by blending the two can be harmful or even deadly if inhaled.

- To avoid falls, wipe up spills and splashed water immediately. Use rubber backed or non-skid rugs in the bathroom.

1. The Bathtub

- Never, never leave your child unattended in the bathtub, not even to answer the phone or the door. Children have drowned in a few inches of water when they been left unattended. If the phone or doorbell rings, ignore it or take the child with you to answer it.

- Keep one hand on the child at all times when you are bathing her. Bath supports for babies who can sit up, while they are helpful, should not be trusted as the babies' sole protection from drowning. Never leave your child unsupervised in water.

- Keep the temperature in the hot water tank at 120F (48C) or lower. Most hot water tanks are kept at 150F (65C). Hot water can cause serious burns in only a second or two. Test the water with your own hand before putting the child into it.

- If you have been drinking alcohol or are on medication that makes you drowsy, don't bathe your child; wait until you are feeling better. You have to be alert, or you are endangering your child.

- If you are tired, and are taking a bath to relax, do not take the baby into the bath with you.

- Pad the tap spout with a sponge or one of the many commercially available spout protectors to help prevent injuries a child might suffer from falling against it. You can purchase pads that come in interesting designs for children.

- Do not let siblings bathe together without adult supervision unless one is old enough to act responsibly.

One terrible incident occurred when an exhausted mother took her infant daughter into the bathtub with her. The baby was lying on the mother's chest. The mother eventually dosed off and the child fell into the water and drowned.

- Use a non-slip mat or non-skid tread tape on the tub floor and don't allow the children to stand up in the tub or on the sides of the tub. Teach them to stay seated in the tub. A fall in a bathtub could easily result in a serious head injury; such a fall could also cause a fractured arm or leg.

- Install a safety grab bar. This is a good idea for young and old alike.

- Keep everything you need to bath a child — washcloths, soap, shampoo, and a favorite bath toy — close to you so you will not be tempted to leave the child to get supplies.

- Bath oil beads are a perfect size to block an airway. They can also be poisonous. Make sure the lids for shampoo and liquid soap are secure and out of your child's reach. Better yet, use products with pumps.

- In whirlpool tubs, keep hands and hair clear of the suction drain. Very young children should not be allowed into a whirlpool or hot tub. Watch older children carefully and do not exceed the recommended time in the water. Children are particularly susceptible to heat-related illnesses. Never leave a child in water unattended.

- Children (and adults, too, for that matter) should avoid sitting directly on the bathtub drain, intestinal injury could result from the suction that is created as water drains away.

2. The Toilet

Children seem to be fascinated with flushing toilets. The noise and the swirling water seems to keep them amazed. Every year a small number of children drown when they fall head first into the toilet. Many more explore toilets. That exploration is obviously unsanitary; it can contribute to the spread of disease.

Toilet Latches

I was called to a home where a child stepped into the toilet and his foot was stuck in the hole at the bottom. We had quite challenge to free his foot.

Keep the following tips in mind for the toilets in your house.

- Use a toilet-lid latch to keep the toilet lid closed.

- Do not use toilet bowl deodorizers or cleaners that hang on the inside of the rim; they are poisonous.

- Chemical toilet bowl cleaners that go into the tank are also poisonous. Avoid them until the children are old enough to know and understand the dangers.

- When your child graduates to toilet training, make sure you have a safe toilet trainer that has non-skid steps and handrails. Toilet training should always be done with adult supervision.

Kids for Keeps

3. The Sink

Until your child is old enough to bathe in the bathtub, the sink is frequently used to bathe infants. Use the same precautions that you would use in a bathtub: lower the water temperature; provide a spout protector; and never leave a child unattended. Here are a few more tips:

- Tighten the taps snugly in the off position. This will make it more difficult for young children to turn the taps on when you are not around.

- Until your child is tall enough to reach the sink, you may want her to use a stool. Make sure the stool is stable and that it has a non-slip surface.

4. Medicine Cabinet, Counters, and Cupboards

One does not have to look too hard to find hazardous products in the bathroom. A few of the dangerous products that are often kept in the bathroom are medications, vitamins, razor blades, cleaning materials, and corrosives. These and other dangerous products must be kept out of the reach of children.

- Remove all potentially dangerous products from the medicine cabinet. Keep them locked in a safe place, or install locks on the medicine cabinet.

- Mouthwash looks pretty and children see you gargle every day. Unfortunately, many mouthwashes contain alcohol. Most young children cannot master gargling; they are liable to drink the mouthwash instead. It does not take much alcohol to give a child an overdose.

- Toothpaste, shampoo, and cream rinses may smell wonderful; they may even taste good, but if they are ingested, they can be poisonous to children. Teach your children not to eat toothpaste or drink shampoo. Consider buying products that are not so appealing to a child's senses.

- Do not keep items such as lipstick, perfume, razors, medications, contact lens solutions, or any other potentially dangerous products on the counter. Put them away immediately after use.

- A razor blade can cut a little face to pieces when young children try to imitate dad shaving. Razors left by the sink can cut little fingers.

- Dangerous products that you have stored under the sink should be removed and kept in a locked closet. If that is not possible, put them on a shelf which is out of the reach of children.

- Glass bottles or cups can fall and break, hurling sharp glass several feet in all directions. Use an unbreakable glass or cup in the bathroom.

- Many electrocutions happen every year when electrical appliances are used in and around water. Unplug your hair dryer and put it away after each use. Keep it and all other electrical appliances well away from water.

The Kitchen

9

You will likely spend many hours in the kitchen with your child. This room is often the scene of injuries both to adults and children alike. If your baby is going to be in the kitchen with you when you are cooking, put him in a playpen away from the stove and other hazards.

When children get older they might want to help you with the cooking. This is a good time to instruct them not only in cooking, but also regarding safe ways to handle knives and the proper procedures to use around the stove and other appliances.

One case I attended involved a five year old boy who wanted to help his mother cook. When she left the kitchen, he reached up over the stove and his baggy sleeve caught fire. The child ran, fanning the flames. The child incurred second and third degree burns on his arm and he faced many weeks of painful treatment in a burn unit.

1. The Stove

- Keep the children away from the stove while you're cooking and well out of your path when you're carrying hot pots. If a pot is dropped, the hot contents could splash a considerable distance.

- Never sit your child on the stove when you are working in the kitchen, even though you are sure the stove is not on. Small children have turned on the stove when their parent wasn't watching, and suffered severe burns to their buttocks and legs.

- Keep the pot handles pointed inward and toward the back of the stove. Try to use the back burners as much as possible. Many scalds happen when a child pulls a pot of hot fluid onto himself.

- A stove guard may help prevent children from reaching the pots on a stove. These are barriers which will surround the elements and make it more difficult for the child to reach the stove top. Some people find these a bother when they are cooking because they reduce the amount of working space on the stove. Whether you choose to use guards is a matter of personal preference.

- Do not store candies and goodies over the stove. Children will eventually climb up to try to reach them.

- Keep the children away when using oven cleaner. It is very poisonous. If you use a self-cleaning oven, remember that the outside of the stove can get just as hot as when the stove is in use; keep your children well away from the unit, whichever method you use to clean it.

- Most house fires start in the kitchen. The kitchen is a good place to have a fire extinguisher. Learn how and when to use it. Locate it in a readily accessible place and read the manufacturer's instructions for installation and use.

2. Other Kitchen Appliances

Kitchen appliances have been the cause of many injuries, ranging from burns from microwave ovens to poisoning from dishwasher detergent. With a bit of caution, many injuries can be prevented.

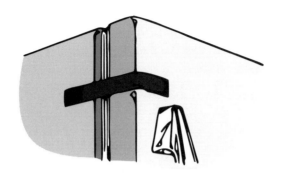

Appliance Latch

- Appliance latches will help to keep children from opening doors to the refrigerator and dishwasher. There are several types. One variety on the market requires that one part of the latch be attached to the appliance and the other be attached to the appliance door; the two parts latch together when the door is closed. Other types use Velcro to secure the door. Neither of these latches is fool proof, so you will still want to keep dangerous products that require refrigeration (such as medicines and vitamins) in a safe place.

- Refrigerators manufactured in Canada and the U.S.A. must open from the inside. However, it is still possible to find old refrigerators in operation that cannot be opened from the inside. These refrigerators have turned into coffins that have caused death by suffocation when they have been discarded outside and children have climbed in and closed the door. If there is one in your area, the door should be removed and it should be disposed of appropriately.

- If you have a freezer, it should be kept locked. The key should be kept in a safe place out of reach of children. This is another appliance in which children have died from freezing or suffocation.

- Fridge magnets can fall off onto the floor and become yet another object within reach that could cause choking.

- The dishwasher door should be secured so that its contents cannot be reached by a child. Dishwasher detergent is poisonous. It should be kept in a safe place and not added to the machine until you are ready to start it.

- Keep items such as toasters, electric kettles, and blenders away from the edge of the counter so that they are difficult for children to pull down onto themselves. Keep them unplugged when they are not being used.

- When heating milk or food in the microwave, make sure you test it for temperature before giving it to your baby. The food may be very hot at its core, yet not appear to be hot on its surface. Shake a baby bottle before testing the milk on your wrist.

3. The Table, Counters, Drawers, and Cupboards

- Most kitchen drawers contain potentially harmful items and should have safety latches. These are inexpensive devices which will make it more difficult for a child to open the drawer. It is important that you make sure to close the drawer all the way, activating the latch.

- Cabinets with potentially harmful products in them should have cabinet latches. These should give good protection against a child's inquisitive nature. Remember, though, that these latches are not fool proof! With enough persistence, children might be able to figure out how they work.

- Avoid using table cloths. It is very easy for a child to pull on them and have everything on the table swept onto the floor — and the child. Using placemats instead of a full table cloth will help to reduce this hazard.

- Many burns have happened when a baby was sitting on someone's knee at the table when hot coffee or tea was spilled.

- Don't leave hot pots or dishes on the table or counter where a baby might be able to reach them.

- Don't leave knives on the counter when children are close by. Many knife incidents have happened when a parent was distracted for just a second or two. Use knives and sharp objects carefully, and for their intended purpose only. Always work in good light.

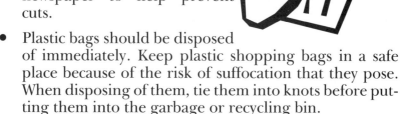

- The garbage bin should have a lid on it. When disposing of objects such as broken glass or light bulbs, wrap them up in newspaper to help prevent cuts.

- Plastic bags should be disposed of immediately. Keep plastic shopping bags in a safe place because of the risk of suffocation that they pose. When disposing of them, tie them into knots before putting them into the garbage or recycling bin.

- Dispensers for aluminum foil, plastic wrap, and wax paper have sharp serrated edges. Keep them out of reach or in a drawer with a safety latch.

- Toothpicks are responsible for many injuries every year. They are sharp and can injure eyes and cause cuts to mouths and throats. Quite often they are left on a table or counter where a baby or an infant can easily reach them.

4. Highchairs, Hook-on Chairs, and Booster Seats

A. The Highchair

Your child will probably use a highchair from the time she is old enough to sit up unassisted until the time she is tall enough to see over the table from a regular chair.

The Consumer Product Safety Commission estimated that 7,000 children were treated in hospitals in the U.S.A. in one year from injuries involving highchairs.

- A highchair should be sturdy and have a wide base. It should also have a strap-in system with a waist strap and a crotch strap that will help keep the child seated. The strap should be easy to buckle and you must use it every time the child uses the chair. Do not rely on the tray to keep the child secured in the chair.

- Children in highchairs must be supervised. Do not leave them alone.

- If the highchair is placed close to the walls or furniture, it is possible for the child to push off them with his legs, tipping the chair over. Serious injuries may result from a fall from the height of most highchairs.

- If the chair you are using is a folding model, make sure it is locked in place so that it cannot collapse with your baby in it.

- Be careful when lifting the tray up or down and make sure you don't bang your child's head, hurt a little nose, or pinch little fingers.

- Empty chairs can also be a problem. Children have a tendency to climb onto things. If they try to climb onto a chair, the chair may tip over, and it may fall onto the child.

B. Hook-on Chairs

Some parents prefer to use hook-on chairs instead of highchairs. Still other parents have both, using the highchair at home and a hook-on chair when they travel. These chairs usually have a clamp that secures the chair to the edge of the table. Once again, care must be taken when using them.

- Make sure the chair is clamped firmly onto the table before you place your child into it. Follow the manufacturer's instructions carefully, and check the chair every time you use it.

- The chair should have a restraining device to keep the child in the chair.

- The table to which the hook-on chair is attached must be sturdy. Do not attach the chair to glass tables, a table leaf or any kind of flimsy table.

- Hook-on chairs have been knocked off with the child in them when large dogs or siblings have bumped against the chair.

- Do not place a chair under the hook-on seat. The child may try to stand up on it or push off from the chair seat. This could cause the hook-on seat to fall off the table.

- If your child can bounce the chair, it is time to stop using it.

C. Booster Seats

When your child can sit unassisted, he is ready to use these seats safely. The booster seat is designed to sit on the seats of regular chairs. Hazards can occur if the child is active and the booster seat is not secure.

- A child has to be able to sit unassisted to use these seats safely.

- The booster seat should have a strap that will secure the seat to the chair to prevent the seat from sliding off. Check the strap frequently to make sure that it has not slipped or loosened.

- Some seats can be adjusted for height; select a comfortable height for your child.

- Booster seats intended for use in the home are not to be confused with the booster seats designed for use in motor vehicles.

The Living Room and Family Room

10

Most families spend a good part of the day in the living room or family room. Family rooms and living rooms are places of relaxation, entertainment, and socializing, but they can also be full of hazards that may cause injury or even death.

An incident happened when a plant hanging from the ceiling gave way and landed on a child's head. The child died of a severe head injury.

1. Furniture

Family rooms and living rooms are furnished for comfort and enjoyment, yet our choices in furnishing these rooms may present potential hazards — especially for young children. The Consumer Product Safety Commission (CPSC) reported that in the U.S.A. in 1983, coffee tables were the cause of 87,000 injuries; sofas were responsible for 24,000 injuries; and chairs caused 48,000 injuries. The children involved in these injuries were all under four years of age. Here are some tips to make your family and living rooms safer:

- Consider adding well-made, child-sized tables and chairs to your furnishings.

- Make sure the drawers of furniture and cabinets have safety latches that will prevent the drawers from being pulled all the way out.

- Keep dangerous products out of drawers and cabinets that the children can reach.

- Many coffee tables have glass tops. Minute cracks that are very difficult to spot can develop in the glass. These cracks have been known to develop into breaks, which can, in turn, cause serious injury. Children should not be allowed to climb, sit, or stand on these coffee tables. Consider having a piece of safety glass cut to fit the top of your table; it is much harder to break than regular glass.

- Sharp corners on furniture have caused many injuries when children have fallen against them. Pads may be purchased that fit on the edges. Foam may be taped to the corners of furniture; however, you must be careful that the child does not tear off pieces of foam and put them in his mouth, creating a choking hazard.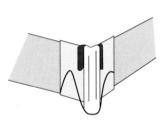

- Upholstered furniture may develop tears; watch for choking hazards from the material. Also check for nails or tacks that have fallen out or are starting to fall out of furniture upholstery.

- Keep items such as medications, cigarettes, lighters, ashtrays, pencils, and scissors off tables. Be careful where you place hot cups; a child might easily pull a cup off the table and spill the scalding liquid on herself.

- Recliner chairs have killed children whose heads have been caught between the foot rest and the chair seat. Fingers and hands have also been broken. You might consider storing your favorite recliner until the children are older. An alternative would be to tie the base of the chair so that it will not open.

Kids for Keeps

- Rocking chairs can crush little hands. Don't let your children play close to them, especially when someone is rocking the chair. Children have injured themselves when they rocked the chair past the safe limit and the chair tipped over backwards.

- Beanbag chairs and infants don't mix. It is possible for an infant to suffocate in a beanbag chair if he rolls over onto his face and is unable to either lift his head or roll onto his back.

- You can reduce the chance of floor lamps being tipped over by keeping them adequately weighted at the base and by positioning them in some inaccessible place behind heavy furniture.

- Position table lamps at the back of tables. This might make it a little more difficult for small children to reach them.

- Remember to use cord shorteners to keep electrical cords out of reach and to keep little hands from pulling on them (see Electricity in *Burns and Scalds, Chapter Six*).

- Try not to place furniture close to windows; the furniture could aid a child in climbing out of your apartment or house. Use window locks to prevent the child from crawling out of the window.

- Keep traffic areas and exits free of furniture and obstructions.

- Don't let the window blind cords dangle within reach of the children; shorten the cord (see Window Blind Cords in *Choking, Suffocation, Strangulation, and Drowning, Chapter Three*).

- If you decide to keep alcohol in the family or living room, it should be stored in a locked cabinet. It takes very little alcohol to cause an overdose in a child.

- Keep the carpet clean and free of debris. Heavily textured carpets can hide tacks, pins, nails, or small objects that could be ingested and cause choking.

- Children have pulled bookshelves down onto themselves and caused themselves serious injuries. Securing shelves properly will help prevent this. Bolt cabinets, bookshelves, and other climbable objects to the wall and secure heavy items, such as television sets, that could be tipped over.

- Electronic equipment — stereos, VCRs, tape decks, compact disc players and televisions — should be positioned where the child cannot knock them over or pull them down onto himself. Keep these machines on sturdy furniture or secured high out of reach. Also remember to secure their cables and cords.

- VCRs have injured many little fingers when those fingers have reached in to explore the unknown. You can purchase guards which fit into the tape slot.

2. The Fireplace

Children are fascinated by fire. Keep children safely away by having a fireplace boundary rule that sounds like this: "You may sit and watch the fire, but stay behind the hearth." Give a limit of safety and stick to it. A fireplace in use is, of course, dangerous because of the fire, but remember that a fireplace hearth has sharp, hard edges that can cause serious damage to a head that comes into contact with it.

- When your child is learning to walk, pad the hearth. You can purchase ready-made padding for this purpose or you can pad it yourself. Make sure whatever you use is not flammable and that it is durable enough to resist tears that would expose the stuffing.

- Do not place furniture so close to the hearth that a child running around or jumping off the furniture could fall into the fireplace or fall onto the hearth. Cushions can be purchased that will help to protect your child from falls on the hearth.

- If you have a gas fireplace, keep the key and igniting devices for the gas out of reach.

- Keep a screen around the fireplace or install glass doors to help keep sparks away from children and furnishings.

- If you have a fire burning in the fireplace, keep the playpen a safe distance from it. The radiating heat from a fireplace is easy to underestimate.

3. Glass, Screen, and Storm Doors

- Children who are running and playing can make the mistake of not seeing the glass on sliding doors and they can run right into it. Don't allow children to run in front of glass doors. Usually it takes quite a bit of force to break the glass, but if it does break, severe lacerations can result. Alternatively, the child could knock herself out. Placing stickers on the glass might help prevent this problem.

- Make sure the screens on screen doors are in good repair. Little fingers and hands seem irresistibly drawn to tears or holes in a screen. While most new screening material is made from plastic mesh, the older wire screen can scratch or cut delicate skin. Large holes could present a head entrapment danger.

- Storm doors often have a sliding glass panel that can be raised to expose a screen. This ventilation feature of a storm door can be dangerous if the sliding glass portion is not properly secured each time it is raised. Children leaning against the screen on the door have had fingers amputated when the heavy glass panel unexpectedly came down.

Adult Bedrooms 11

Your bedroom, your haven. Well, not exactly. When children come into your life, every room in the house is theirs for play, exploration, and potential trouble. Don't neglect to make adult bedrooms as safe as the rest of your home. Because we do not normally associate a place with children doesn't mean that we should not be alert to the possible hazards for a child. Keep this in mind when you consider other areas of the home such as en suite baths, powder rooms, walk-in closets, exercise rooms, and studies.

- Do not leave your purse or briefcase lying around where a child may be able to reach it. The "medicine chest" in your bag could kill a child.

- Don't store your medications, cosmetics, or perfumes on the night table or the dresser where children will easily be able to reach them. Often sleeping children of visitors are placed in an adult's bedroom while their parents are socializing. A curious child can awaken and find medications on night tables or in drawers.

- Remember that in an adult bed, babies can roll off, slip between the wall and the bed, or suffocate in soft bedding. Infants should always be placed on firm, flat surfaces.

- Watch what you put into the trash can. Many harmful items end up in there. Pen caps, hair pins, and coins often fall onto the floor and become potential choking hazards.

- Guns should not be stored in closets. Keep them in a locked area or cabinet, and the keys should be kept well out of children's reach. Guns should be stored unloaded and the ammunition should be stored separately. A trigger lock could further reduce the chance of a dangerous situation.

- Some people keep their exercise machines in the bedroom. Fingers have been amputated by these machines. Keep the children at a safe distance if you are using the machines and away from them when they are not in use. Teach them that this equipment is not a toy or a "ride."

- Remember to tie up blinds and drapery cords, secure all electrical outlets, and shorten or conceal electrical cords.

- Children have pulled down dry-cleaning bags from closets, put them over their head, and suffocated. Remember that over-loaded closet shelves could result in a dangerous avalanche.

- Some dressers and side tables do not require much force to tip if a top drawer is open and and a child pulls down on it. Children can do this easily if they are trying to pull themselves up to see what is inside a drawer. Don't let them play with the dresser.

- Bolt cabinets, bookshelves and other climbable objects to the wall and secure heavy items, such as television sets, that could be tipped over.

The Basement, Workshop, and Laundry Room

12

On rainy days, parents often will send children into the basement recreation rooms to play. This gives children a lot of opportunity to look for and to get into trouble. In most houses you do not have to look very hard to find potential hazards in the basement, workshop, and laundry room: paints, laundry detergent, oils, power tools, and sharp objects are just a few. Washers and dryers are other dangers we have to watch for. Precautions in these areas should heed the old adage that suggests that things that are "out of sight, are out of mind." Hazardous goods and equipment should be properly stored behind locked doors; consider making certain areas "out of bounds" behind safety gates.

I recall when some children found a rifle shell in the house. They took it into the basement, put it into the vice and took the lead out. One of them took a punch and hit the primer with a hammer, setting off some of the leftover gunpowder. The result was that my friend lost part of his finger. I was lucky; I still have all of mine.

1. Basement

- Supervision is a must for children in the basement. If they are left alone, they will eventually get into trouble.

- Sometimes mice or rats will infest a basement. If you have children you may want to consider an alternative to poison. Traps come in a variety of designs, from the spring-loaded mouse trap to traps which will capture the animal alive. Young fingers can be injured in a spring loaded trap, but even a small amount of poison may kill a child (see Poisoning, Chapter Four).

- A major threat in the basement is the furnace, which can be a source of lethal carbon monoxide (CO) poisoning if it is poorly maintained or improperly vented. Each year have all your home heating equipment, flues, and ventilation systems checked and maintained. Keep the heating equipment clean, including filters and vents to the outside. Consider installing a carbon monoxide detector alongside the smoke detector.

2. Workshop

- Obviously, power tools can be dangerous. You should always practice the appropriate safety techniques. Hand tools require an equal amount of care. Set a good example for your child: use safety goggles to prevent eye injuries from flying particles. If your child wishes to watch you work, make sure she has a pair too.

- A toddler may have his own play tools and may not understand that it is dangerous to play with real tools. It is your responsibility to make sure tools are out of your children's reach and that they are taught not to touch them.

- Avoid poor lighting, wet floors, and clutter. Be especially alert to the unsafe storage of dangerous substances. Flammable or combustible products, such as paint, turpentine, or linseed oil require extra care with their use and with their storage. Rags soaked in these chemicals could ignite by themselves; dispose of them promptly and correctly.

3. Laundry Room

- Teach your children that washers and dryers are not toys and should not be played with. Many children have died in washers or dryers. When the machines are not in use, keep their lids closed.

- They are hard to find now, but the old ringer washing machines were the cause of many hands and arms being broken or crushed when they were caught in the ringer.

- As unlikely as it may sound, pets should not be put into washers and dryers. There are other ways of dealing with the dirty or wet kitten even though the child saw that her mother washed a soiled teddy bear in the washer. In other words, be sure children understand what is and what is not appropriate to put into laundry machines.

- It should be possible to open the dryer from the inside just in case a child finds his way inside. Always check inside a laundry machine before turning it on.

Children have have hidden in clothes dryers and died. In one case I attended, a 9 year-old boy was playing in the dryer. He had one leg in the drum when his sister pushed the start button; the result was a broken leg.

- Wash tubs should not be left with water in them; drownings have occurred when children have fallen in.

- Washing detergents and bleach are poisonous. They also can cause chemical burns to the mouth and esophagus (the tube that carries food from the mouth to the stomach). Detergent powders can cause breathing difficulties. Dispose of all empty detergent boxes quickly; if a child puts his hand into a detergent box and then into his mouth, serious complications may result.

- Make sure hot irons are kept away from little hands. The iron's cord almost always hangs off the ironing board. If the iron is pulled off the board, it could easily land on your child's head or cause a burn.

- When putting away an ironing board, make sure there are not little fingers close to the collapsing legs.

The Yard and Garage

13

M any of the incidents that injure children happen in and around the yard. Various mishaps can happen in the yard and garage when a parent is doing spring cleanup or working on the motor vehicle. It is very hard to fix the motor vehicle or do yard work while watching the children. In the majority of injury situations in or around the home, a common factor is the lack of supervision. After, the parents said they took their eyes off the children for "just a second."

Your backyard play areas should follow the same guidelines for safety that are mentioned in the playground safety chapter (Playgrounds, Chapter Fifteen). Falls, strangulation, head entrapment and head injuries are a few of the injuries that can happen on swing sets and in other play areas.

Personal swimming pools, hot tubs, and trampolines are frequently found in the back yards of family homes and I have included discussions of them in this chapter.

1. Yard Hazards

Your child will probably spend a significant amount of time in the yard. Supervision for young children playing in a yard is very important. If possible, your yard should be fenced. Many of the hazards in a yard result from poor yard maintenance. Young children especially will try to put anything they find into their mouths. Take a good look around, and put away or fix any hazards you find.

- Fences are a great idea to help keep your children in the yard, and other children and animals out. They can be a great assistance in helping to prevent children from gaining access to the street. But you have to remember that children can climb fences. Children can also open gates, so there is no guarantee that your children will not leave a fenced yard.

- Identify the types of plants you have in the yard to determine if they are poisonous. Once you know what they are, you can call the Poison Control Center in your area to see if they are in fact poisonous (see Poisoning, Chapter Four).

- Don't allow your children to play in areas where you have just used horticultural sprays or powders. Some lawn and garden products are highly toxic, with toddlers and pets at highest risk during their frolics in the grass. Read and heed the manufacturer's warnings concerning fertilizers, insecticides, and weed killers.

- Cut sharp branches which are at eye level or lower. Eyes have been poked out when children have run into such hazards.

- Clean up pet droppings as soon as possible. Cover your sandbox. You don't want your children digging up the neighborhood cat feces.

- Clean up cigarette butts. They are not healthy for children or anyone else.

- Make garbage cans inaccessible; they not only cause odor but they also harbor bacteria.

- Make sure nails, screws, and other sharp objects are picked up. This could prevent a trip to the hospital for your child or yourself.

- Take a good look at your deck to see if there are places where small heads could become entrapped.

- If you have a wood pile, be sure it is stable and won't fall down on a child. Children sometimes find these piles fascinating places to play.

- Make sure that neither bees nor wasps are building a nest in the wood pile or anywhere else in your yard. Fatalities have resulted when children and adults have unintentionally stumbled upon a wasp nest.

- If you have a backyard fire pit, make sure your children and other children visiting respect fire and stay clear of the fire pit.

- When barbecues are in use, they are hot! Make sure your children will not be able to come into contact with a barbecue in use. Keep them at a safe distance.

- More than two-thirds of the children injured by lawn mowers were bystanders; more than three-quarters of those hurt required amputation (mostly toes and feet), according to the American Orthopedic Foot and Ankle Society.

- Lawn mowers can pick up and throw stones, nails, pieces of wire, or other debris at a very high rate of speed. Keep your children away from the danger by keeping them away from the lawn mower until they are old enough to understand how dangerous it can be.

- Similar dangers to those encountered with lawn mowers are present when you are using hedge trimmers and snow-blowers. Keep children and all bystanders well away from flying debris.

- Falls from trees are a common injury in back yards. Unintentional hangings can also happen. Do not let children play with ropes around trees.

2. Swimming Pools and Hot Tubs

Working as a paramedic I have personally been involved with several drownings that have occurred in backyard pools. If you have a pool, constant supervision is critical when there are children around.

- Make sure the fence will keep out the neighbors' children. Keep your gate locked when the pool is not in use. The height of the fence should be a minimum of 5 feet and you should use a self-locking gate.

- Sliding doors from the house to the pool deck should be locked to avoid having children get out to the pool area unsupervised.

- Consider a pool alarm. These are devices that float in the pool; the rocking motion caused by sudden waves will sound the alarm. This warns you that someone may have fallen in. Remember, an alarm does not prevent children from falling in, it only warns you after the event — don't rely on it.

- Avoid running and horseplay on the pool deck. Decks are usually slippery and they are always hard.

- Diving boards may be dangerous in certain pools. Many broken necks have been the result of hitting the upslope of the pool bottom head first. This is also a frequent cause of spinal cord injuries in adolescents and adults.

- Pool covers do not prevent drownings. In fact, children and adults have drowned when they became trapped under the pool cover and could not get out.

- Children may drown in pools of water that have collected on top of the pool cover after a rain. When there is a small weight on the cover (such as a small child), the water will collect in the indentation and form a puddle that is deep enough to drown a small child.

- Covers for hot tubs should be locked to keep children out.

- In a hot tub, close supervision is as important as it is for swimming pools. Very young children should not be allowed into hot tubs. Young children cannot tolerate the heat as well as adults can; serious heat-related illnesses may occur.

- Keep pool and hot tub chemicals out of reach of the children and locked in a cabinet.

102

3. Trampolines

Trampolines have the potential to cause serious injuries. A combination of skilled instruction, adequate supervision, proper clothing, and the use of a safety harness can help to reduce injuries, although injuries have still occurred even when all the safety precautions have been followed. Parents must be aware of these facts:

- Maneuvers such as somersaults have a high potential to cause serious injuries. They should only be attempted under the training and supervision of a skilled instructor.

- Trampolines must be secured when not in use and must be well maintained.

- Collisions can result in injury if more than one person is on the trampoline. Enforce the rule that there should only be one person at a time on the trampoline.

- You can be held liable for injuries sustained by other children using your trampoline.

Bounce and Break

4. Garage Safety

The garage is a place where children are attracted to play with their friends. There are many dangers to be found there: anti-freeze, gasoline, matches, and sharp tools. Children should be taught that the garage is not a place to play and children always should be supervised if they are in a garage.

In the U.S.A. between 1985 and 1988, twenty-five deaths were caused from automatic garage door openers. Nearly all of those fatalities were children under 8 years of age (Consumer Product Safety Commission).

- If you have an automatic garage door opener, make sure it has an automatic reverse and that this feature is functioning. This will open the door if it comes into contact with any resistance. The automatic garage door switch should be out of children's reach.

- Make sure there are no children playing in the driveway when you are parking or backing up your motor vehicle. Too many times a parent or visitor has backed up over a child.

- Sharp garden tools such as garden forks, rakes, hoes, edgers, and hedge clippers can turn into very dangerous weapons when children swing them about. If you see this starting to happen, put a stop to it immediately. Store garden tools safely out of a child's reach.

- Electric tools, extension cords, and unprotected socket plugs are a potentially deadly combination in your garage. Make sure power tools and cords are securely stored. Don't neglect to put socket protectors on garage and other outdoor power sources.

- Children have started fires by playing with gasoline or other flammable liquids stored in the garage.

- Never store flammable or toxic chemicals in pop bottles; a young child may be tempted to drink them.

- Many motor vehicle cleaning products are stored in the garage. Make sure they are safely stored and out of the reach of children.

Kids for Keeps

Playing Outdoors   **14**

P laying outdoors is one of the great joys of childhood, and playing with your child outdoors is one of the great joys of parenthood. However, keeping your kids safe outside takes almost as much thought as keeping them safe in your home. This chapter is about some of the hazards one finds in the natural environment. With a little forethought, exploring the world with our children can be exciting and safe.

This chapter discusses some of the hazards to children to be found outside your home. The medical profession has made us increasingly aware of the dangers of exposure to the sun's radiation. Heat-induced illnesses are especially critical to youngsters. Insect and animal bites (which can take place indoors or outdoors, though more frequently take place outdoors) are usually more devastating for children than adults.

Allergic reactions to substances in the environment can take place almost anywhere, and so I have devoted a whole chapter to them (see Chapter Five). The chapter following this one specifically addresses safety on playgrounds.

1. The Sun and Sunscreens

I'm sure we can all remember times during the summer holidays when we would fry our little bodies in the sun until we were lobster red, then go home and cry for an hour or two at night because it hurt. In the days of our childhood we weren't aware of the serious health risks that a sunburn can bring; now, as parents, we are.

As we become more aware of the hazards of exposure to the ultraviolet (UV) rays of the sun, we have to keep in mind that a child's skin is more sensitive than that of adults. Many pediatricians recommend that children should not be directly exposed to the sun for the entire first year of their life. Check with your own physician for advice.

Make your child aware of the hazards of exposure to the sun. Here are some very good routines for them to develop in childhood that will serve them for life.

- Don't expose your child to midday sun. Avoid being in the sun between 11:00 a.m. and 2:00 p.m.

- It is possible to burn even on a cloudy day. As much as 80% of the sun's UV rays can reach the earth even when it is overcast.

- With an increase in elevation, the radiation from the sun also increases. Take extra care if you are going to the mountains.

- If children are taken outdoors, proper clothing such as wide-brimmed hats, long-sleeved shirts, and long pants should be worn. Your child's sun hat should cover all of the head and neck area. Tightly woven, light colored fabrics will help prevent sunburn.

- Sunscreen should not be applied to infants under 6 months of age; therefore, they should not be exposed to the sun.

- After six months of age, your child should be covered with sunscreen that has protection against UV-A and UV-B. Some specialists recommend that the sunscreen have no less than a SPF 15 rating. The SPF rating is found on all sunscreen or sunblock lotions and creams; the higher the SPF, the greater the protection. SPF products of up to 60 are now available.

- Some people are allergic to the ingredient PABA found in some sunscreens. Your physician or pharmacist can give you advice on a suitable sunscreen.

Kids for Keeps

- Apply the sunscreen 15 to 30 minutes before going out into the sun. This will allow it to penetrate into the lower layers of the skin. Repeat application every 60 to 90 minutes. Carefully read the instructions for applying sunscreen or sunblock.

- If children are playing in or near water, on snow, dry sand, or concrete, remember that these surfaces reflect light and the risk of sun burn is therefore increased. The brighter the surface, the more UV is reflected. Water can also reduce or remove some sunscreens.

- Remember that no sunscreen offers total protection from all the sun's rays. If you stay out long enough, you'll burn.

- Certain medications can increase the skin's sensitivity to sunlight. Check for this factor with your physician.

2. Heat-Induced Illnesses

As children get older, their mobility increases. They tend to have an endless supply of energy. Sometimes this can get them into trouble in hot weather. When children play hard in hot temperatures, they can sometimes develop signs of heat exhaustion, heat cramps, and possibly heat stroke, which is a life-threatening condition. Children are more prone to these conditions than adults. Sometimes they do not pay enough attention to the warning signs; you need to. The following tips may help prevent heat-induced illnesses.

- On very hot days (especially hot, humid days) do not allow children to over-exert themselves. Avoid the sun between 11:00 a.m. and 2:00 p.m.

In Arizona a small child fell on the asphalt and was not able to stand up. This resulted in burns so serious that the child required hospitalization.

- Have children drink plenty of water before, during, and after playing. Explain to them that water is very good for them. Remember, when a child says she is thirsty, it is already past the best time to re-hydrate.

- If a child starts to feel weak, dizzy, or ill, have him stop what he is doing and move him to a cool, shady place. If the child is not yours, his parents or guardian should be notified.

- Remember that heat illnesses can happen without playing directly in the sun. For example, the inside of a car can reach very high temperatures in a very short time when parked in the hot sun with the windows closed (see Chapter Seventeen, *Motor Vehicle Safety*).

- On hot sunny days common objects can become hot enough to burn a child. Motor vehicle seats left in the sun, tar on a road, metal lawn chairs, or even toys left in the sun can be the source of burns.

3. Winter Safety

Many of the precautions you should take when going outdoors on a sunny day apply to taking your child outdoors on wintery days — the obvious difference is that cold days require appropriately warm clothing, such as hats, mittens, and boots. Here are some additional tips for making winter outings safe:

- Dress children in layers.

- If children are playing on snow, remember that it reflects light and the risk of sun burn is therefore increased. Use sunscreen on exposed skin, especially in the mountains.

- If they are playing in the snow on bright days, children should wear appropriate eye protection: sunglasses or goggles with UV protection.

- A good portion of body heat is lost through the top of the head; make sure your child wears a hat, toque, or hood.

- Children should use footwear that keeps their feet warm and dry.

- Monitor local temperatures and wind chill factors.

- It's a good idea not to expose your children to cold for too lengthy a time. Know the signs of frostbite — a whitening of the skin on the nose, ears, and extremities — and bring your child into a warm shelter before these signs appear!

4. Insect, Bee, and Wasp Stings

In the summer, insects, bees, and wasps can be found almost anywhere. Some summers seem to have more of one variety of insect than others. The results of getting stung can range from a sting that produces a bit of mild discomfort to one that produces a life-threatening condition called *anaphylaxis (see* Chapter Five, *Allergic Reactions).*

Every year people die from bee or wasp stings. If a person is highly allergic to a sting, this can happen from a single sting or from multiple stings — perhaps after a person has stumbled upon a nest. Here are a few tips to consider if you have bees or wasps in your area:

- If you or your child is allergic to bee stings, contact your physician about obtaining a bee sting kit. A person with this allergy should also wear a medi-alert bracelet.

- Wasps and bees like sweet things. Injuries have resulted when a person was eating something sweet and a wasp landed on the food just as the person put the food in his mouth. Stings in the mouth are extremely painful. If there are wasps around, teach your children to look at their food carefully every time they take a bite.

One summer, while returning from camping, where there seemed to have been an unusually large number of wasps, my family stopped at a restaurant. When we started travelling again, my daughter wanted the can of pop that she had started earlier. Realizing that wasps are attracted to sweet things, my wife checked the can for wasps. Sure enough, there was one inside the can. The wasp and the contents of the can were unceremoniously dumped along the highway.

- Bees will be attracted to glasses and cans of pop or beer. Make sure these insects do not crawl into the can unnoticed. You can purchase special reusable can lids to prevent insects from crawling through the pop-top opening.

- Wasps can build nests in your yard which you might not notice. Some of the more popular spots are in trees, in wood piles, under steps, and on or in buildings. Some nest in the ground. Usually nests can be destroyed with commercially available sprays; a professional exterminator will be glad to get rid of the pests for you. Remember to heed all warnings that accompany the use of pesticides (See Chapter Thirteen, *The Yard and Garage*).

- If someone has been stung and is starting to have reactions such as raised welts, swelling, or shortness of breath, seek medical help immediately.

5. Cat and Dog Bites

Pets can be a good source of companionship to a child. If you have a pet, let your child be actively involved in its care. Even young children can learn responsibility for a pet and how to treat animals with love and respect. Almost all children love to handle and play with a puppy or a kitten. However, sometimes young children do not seem to be able to tell the difference between the cute little puppy you have at home, and the large stray dog that walks into your yard or the playground. This could mean trouble.

In the U.S.A., one report showed that there were 157 deaths due to dog bites from 1979 to 1988; 70% of these deaths were children under ten years of age.

Dog bites are a common injury to children; quite often it is the family's dog or a dog that the child is familiar with that does the damage. Strange dogs have also bitten children when a child walked up to pat the dog. All too often when a child is attacked by a dog, it is in the facial area. Severe damage can be done in a split second. You must supervise small children around any dog.

In Canada between April 1990 and April 1992, The Children's Hospital Injury Research and Prevention Program (CHIRPP) reported 1,022 records of injuries from dog bites in children up to 19 years of age (Edmonton Board of Health, Childhood Injury Control Newsletter 1.1, 1989).

A large old dog, known in the neighborhood as a friendly dog, inexplicably bit a child at a school bus stop. This was very surprising to everybody because the dog had always been so friendly. The dog was put down and an autopsy was performed to determine if there was a reason why the dog turned on and bit the child. The autopsy had a surprising result. The skin of the dog had hundreds of needles stuck in it. Apparently children had been sticking needles into the dog for a period of time.

Beware of the Child!

From a very early age children should be instructed on how to handle themselves around dogs and cats. Here is some information you should teach your children:

- Many children have been bitten by their own dogs and cats. Additionally, cats can inflict deep and painful scratches with their claws.

- If you know the animal, stop and let it come to you. Always be gentle in your voice, touch, and movement around an animal. If the animal doesn't come to you, leave it alone.

- Never approach strange dogs or cats — even if the animal is on a leash. Keep close watch on children when dogs or cats are in the same vicinity. Avoid contact with free roaming animals.

- Teach your child about any dangerous neighborhood animals and avoid routes where dogs are known to chase pedestrians or cyclists.

- If a dog does approach your child, teach the child not to panic, but to stand still with hands at sides. Let the dog sniff and speak in a calm low voice to the animal. The dog will probably move away and the child can then also move away.

- Do not approach dogs or cats quickly; you may startle them and their natural response may be to run, or worse, to attack.

- If a dog starts to growl or show signs of aggression, back away. Do not run, or you may trigger the dog's natural chase instinct. Do the same if a cat begins snarling, hissing, and arching its back.

- If children come across a dog in a yard and it is fenced in, do not let children stick their fingers or hands through the fence to pet the dog.

- Don't pull on a cat or dog's tail, ears, or neck — or physically harass the animal in any way. Teach children not to tease dogs or cats with sticks, food, or any other objects. Older children can be taught the fine line between teasing and playing with an animal, and learn the warning signs when playing turns into something more dangerous.

- If a child is bitten by a dog or cat, seek medical aid as soon as possible. Try to remember the circumstances of the attack, the description of the animal, and if possible, obtain the owner's name and address. Later, when you speak to the owner, try to ascertain whether the animal is current in its rabies vaccinations. All of this information may be useful in treating the injuries.

6. Ferret Bites

In the last 10 or 15 years many people have been keeping ferrets as pets. In the U.S.A. there were approximately 50,000 ferrets sold every year. While still classified as wild animals by the U.S. Centers for Disease Control and the American Veterinary Medical Association, none of the provisions of the Wild Life Act in Alberta apply to them. Ferrets can be a hazard to the safety of infants and young children. Some facts about ferrets include these:

- There is no effective vaccine against rabies in ferrets.
- Many health departments recommend that if you have a ferret and young children, you should get rid of the ferret.

Ferret: Mustela putorius

alias ... Escape Artist

- A ferret can inflict hundreds of bites in a very short time. A ferret can bite so aggressively that it might have to be killed or pried off to loosen its hold. The bites may cause severe bleeding leading to death.

- Injuries to infants often involve the face and have resulted in mutilation of the child's ears and nose. In some cases ferrets have jumped into infant cribs and bitten sleeping children.

- If you are visiting someone who has a ferret, be extremely careful; do not allow your child near the ferret.

Playground Safety   **15**

P laygrounds are for play — safe play. Yet tragically every
year children are injured or killed on playgrounds. How
can we ensure our child's safety while she is playing on a playground?

Dr. Patrick Pierse, pediatrician at Edmonton's Grey Nuns
Hospital, says, "We physicians treat too many children who suffer broken bones, sprains, and frightening head injuries after
their playground play. Many of the injuries could be prevented
with supervision, safer surfacing, and equipment. Supervision is
a lifeline to preventing disabling or life-threatening injuries or
even death. I can't stress enough how important it is to be vigilant when supervising."

Supervision, safe playground surfaces, and safe equipment
are the keys to a safer playground. This chapter discusses supervision and safe play, safety on equipment, and prevention for
some of the common injuries on playgrounds. For a more extensive look at the topic, I recommend an excellent book enti-
tled *Removing Playground Hazards for Our Children's Sake*,
published by SAFE KIDS of Alberta and the Alberta Medical Association, much of the following information was taken from this
source.

1. Supervision and Safe Play

A two and a half year-old child and two four year-olds died when their heads got caught between a guard rail and the platform of climbing equipment on a public playground. In each of these three cases, the children were either sitting on the platform with their legs dangling over the edge or else they were lying face down on the platform. The children then slid off the platform under the guard rail, got their heads trapped and died by strangulation.

Playground injuries are preventable — supervision is the key. On the playground, all preschoolers and children should be closely and carefully supervised.

- Check out the playgrounds in your community — shop around until you find one that is safe and be sure that your child is supervised while playing there.

- Adults should examine not only the playground equipment, but also the grounds themselves — is the area free of used condoms, needles, and other foreign matter that could pose a serious health risk if a child picked it up?

- Supervising adults should choose a vantage point at or near high-risk pieces of equipment, particularly slides. Watch for unsafe situations and correct them immediately.

- Pay special attention to what children wear to the playground and make sure that they are dressed appropriately. Avoid clothing with drawstrings, scarves, ties, or loose clothing. Loose tie strings on hoods and scarves around necks can catch on slides and other play equipment and cause strangulation (see Chapter Three, *Choking, Suffocation, Strangulation and Drowning*).

Kids for Keeps

*In June 1992, a two and a half year-old child in Alberta stran-
gled to death on a day care slide when her jacket drawstring
snagged the top of a slide. Three months later, a six year-old
girl in Ontario died the same way.*

- Ensure equipment is appropriate for the children's ages and skills. Make sure your child is not using equipment beyond his or her physical ability.

- Be alert to badly positioned, unstable equipment and debris in the play area.

- Regularly examine your child's playground equipment for sharp edges, protrusions, pinch points, and equipment failures. Check equipment regularly for loose bolts, nuts, and clamps.

- Be aware that equipment in direct sunlight may have hot surfaces.

- Take the weather into account. Wet hands, shoes, or equipment increases the risk of injury.

- Examine the protective surfacing under play equipment. The surface should be a shock-absorbing surface such as sand or pea gravel, not concrete, asphalt, or hard-packed dirt.

- Enforce rules of safe play with your children.

Teach your children these lessons about safety on the playground. A healthy and happy playground experience is more likely if you insist on safe play that includes these simple rules:

- Wear shoes at all times when outside.

- Do not run or play with a sucker, a popsicle stick, or food in your mouth.

- No pushing, shoving, or horseplay on the playground or its equipment.

- Make room for others.

- Stay away from the front and back of swings or other moving parts.
- Keep fingers away from moving parts.
- Beware: equipment is slippery when wet.
- Always hold hand grips and rails.
- Never jump from unsafe heights and always look before jumping.
- Use slides to slide down; do not walk up slides.
- Stop younger children from climbing to unsafe heights.

2. Safety Tips for Playground Equipment

A. Slides

- Use the steps; never climb up the sliding surface or on top of the tunnel.
- Be sure everyone is out of the way before sliding.
- Slide down feet first, sitting up, one person at a time.

B. Swings

- Sit in the center of the seat — never stand or kneel.
- Hold onto the swing with both hands.
- Stop the swing before getting off.
- Only one person at a time on the swing.
- Never swing empty swings.
- Stay away from both the front and the back of moving swings.
- Don't climb the bars of the swing set.

C. Climbing Structures

- Choose a climber appropriate to your child's level of development. If a child must stand on a box to reach a climber or if that child needs to be lifted, he or she is too small for it.

- When several children are playing on horizontal bars and ladders, ensure that they start at the same end and move in the same direction, keeping a safe distance between each of them and watching for swinging feet.

- No overcrowding is allowed on a climber.

- Use the proper grip — the thumb should encircle the bar opposite the fingers.

- Hold on with both hands, except while moving to a new position.

- No speed contests are allowed on climbers.

- Don't try to cover a large distance in a single move.

- To drop, land on your feet with your knees slightly bent.

- Only play on dry structures.

- Do not wear loose-fitting clothing while using the climber.

School Break!

3. Falls on the Playground

Nine out of ten serious injuries to children — mainly head injuries and fractures — are caused by falls on playground surfaces. Protective surfacing cannot prevent all injuries from falls, but it can help reduce both the number and seriousness of injuries.

Examine the protective surfacing under all playground equipment. Surfaces should be soft, shock-absorbing, and resilient. Concrete, asphalt, or hard-packed dirt are inappropriate surfaces for playgrounds. Sand or pea gravel can greatly reduce injuries.

4. Injuries from Arm Swinging

When playing outside with small children, many adults will pick them up by their arms and forcefully swing them around. Most adults will have had this done to them when they were children, and many have done this to a child. Because this is such a common practise, sometimes we fail to realize that injuries can happen from swinging a child by the arms.

A common type of injury due to arm swinging is dislocation of the shoulder or the elbow. When a child is being swung around or picked up by the arms, there is a great deal of force applied to the developing elbows and shoulders. This force may result in the joints popping out of place. The consequences can be especially serious because the child's nerves and arteries can be injured, resulting in permanent damage. To avoid these types of injuries, don't swing children by the arms.

5. Preventing Strangulation on the Playground

Strangulations on playgrounds often result from children getting entangled in playground equipment. Head and neck entrapment is a major cause of strangulation on playgrounds. It typically occurs when a young child's head is placed into an opening, the child's body changes direction, and the child's head cannot be withdrawn. Reversing this kind of incident, we can see when a child's legs pass through an opening and the child's body slips through, the child's head can become trapped. The result is the same: the child is at risk of strangulation.

Supervise your children. Many strangulation incidents can be eliminated if an alert adult is nearby. Here are some tips for preventing strangulation on playground equipment:

- Strangulation occurs when a child's clothing gets caught on equipment, often slides or swings. Be especially vigilant with these devices (see Chapter Three, *Choking, Suffocation, Strangulation and Drowning*).

- A child's scarf, mittens, jacket strings, or jacket hood can become trapped in the small gaps between equipment pieces, the tops of slides, on vertical posts and on the connecting links or S-hooks of chains. Dress your child so that her clothing will not get caught on the playground equipment; remove strings and loose parts from children's clothing.

- Make sure gaps in equipment cannot snare a child's clothing or body. Seal equipment gaps with silicone. Renovate, replace, or discard dangerous pieces of equipment.

- Children can become entangled in ropes, jump ropes, free-hanging ropes, and leashes either inappropriately attached to equipment, or worn around the child's neck.

- Although helmets are important pieces of protective equipment, be aware of the dangers of wearing them on the playground. Strangulations have occurred because helmets became trapped between rungs on climbing equipment.

Recreational Equipment and Vehicle Safety

16

Children and toys: they just go together. Once your child has graduated from the stroller and playpen set and left behind all the equipment of babyhood, a whole new set of equipment will invade your household. Ice skates, hockey sticks, basketballs, rollerblades, skateboards, skis, sleds, baseball gloves, life jackets, soccer balls, and football helmets will begin to fill up the house. New interests for children bring new responsibilities for parents.

Organized sports usually have a set of safety rules and equipment that are taught by coaches and teams. Other sports are based more on individual effort and some of these recreations are the subject of this chapter. For these recreational activities, parents need to learn, teach, and practice safety rules with their children.

In this chapter, I address some fundamental safety concerns in using various types of equipment: toboggans, sleds, in-line skates, skateboards, snowboards, and skis. I also discuss some of the safety issues in using recreational vehicles such as boats, all-terrain vehicles (ATVs) and snowmobiles. There is much information to convey about bicycling, and I have devoted a separate chapter of Bicycle Safety (see Chapter Eighteen).

Because of the activities I discuss in this chapter involve mobility and speed, I stress the use of the correct helmet for the activity. Research shows that, except for high-speed impacts, the proper helmet limits injury in almost every case. Not all helmets are created equal; you should always use the appropriate helmet for a given activity. Bicycle and hockey helmets should carry a seal of approval by the Canadian Standards Association (CSA). Additional seals of approval may come from the American National Standards Institute (ANSI), or the American Society for Testing and Material (ASTM), or the private Snell Memorial Foundation. (For some general observations about helmets, see "Bicycle Helmets" in *Bicycle Safety*, Chapter Eighteen.)

Put quite simply, helmets protect brains. Doctors graphically describe the brain as a Jell-O-like mass that sits in a "bowl" of bone — the skull. As Dr. Robert van Mastrigt, a neuropsychologist and coordinator of the brain injury rehabilitation program at Alberta Children's Hospital said, "When you hit something with speed, your skull stops, your body stops, but that Jell-O in the bowl continues to move with the same force." The still-moving brain can bruise itself against the walls of the skull. At accelerated speeds, the "shearing" forces at impact can tear the brain's tissues, blood vessels, and nerve connections. In extreme situations, the brain stem itself is separated, and that results in a fatality. Dr. Mastrigt's clear message is that "What needs to be understood is that most injuries to the brain can probably be minimized or avoided altogether by the wearing of a helmet" (Calgary Herald, Feb. 5, 1995, p. A3).

As is true of other activities, supervision, training, and appropriate equipment go a long way toward creating a safe environment for your children as they engage in recreational activities. Helmets are essential for many of these sports. Make sure your child has the right helmet, that it fits, and, most importantly, that the child wears it. Remember, set a good example by following the same rules for helmets and equipment that you set for your child.

1. Rollerblades (In-Line Skates)

Rollerblading is also called in-line skating because of the design of the rollers. While regular roller-skates have two pairs of wheels beside each other, the rollers on rollerblades are in a straight line: hence the name, in-line skates. This makes the skates much faster than regular roller skates. In the past few years the sport has become very popular, and because of its popularity there has been an increase of skating injuries. These injuries can range from minor to very severe (Childhood Injury Control #5.3, Edmonton Board of Health).

- When you buy in-line skates you should automatically buy protective equipment. This equipment includes: an approved bicycle helmet, wrist guards, and knee and elbow pads. Don't start skating until you have *all the equipment.*

- Wear a long sleeved shirt and pants or leggings when rollerblading.

In-Line Skating

- Have the child take lessons on proper techniques, such as how to fall safely, how to keep speed in check and how to stop.

- Start skating on a flat surface; three quarters of in-line skating injuries occur on sloped surfaces.

- Skate in daylight and dry conditions.

- Skate in areas that are free of traffic, crowds, debris, and surface irregularities. Avoid pedestrians, motor vehicles, and dogs.

- Do not wear headphones when you are in-line skating.

2. Skateboards and Snowboards

Skateboarding is another sport growing in popularity with older children. Snowboarding is a "crossover sport" from skateboarding. Snowboards obviously have no wheels and are intended for a different terrain, but they work on much the same principles of motion and control as a skateboard. Fractures are the most

Snow Boarding

Kids for Keeps

common injuries with these boards. Frequently arms are fractured in skateboarding when the rider loses control and falls on an outstretched arm. These safety tips may help reduce injury:

- Parents should be aware that these sports are currently in vogue and have a certain fashionable code of dress which does not include the use of helmets. This is one code that both smart parents and young athletes will break. Helmets save lives — period.

- Wear the proper protective equipment; this includes an approved helmet, gloves, knee and elbow pads, and sturdy shoes when skateboarding. Snowboarding requires the use of a helmet and appropriate footwear for either carving boards (which require hard ski boots) or free-style boards (requiring soft shoes designed especially for snowboarding).

- Wear appropriate eye protection for the weather conditions to ensure clear visibility: sunglasses or snow goggles with UV protection assist your vision. Don't forget the sunscreen.

- Skateboard on a smooth and dry surface that is clear of holes, bumps, and rocks. Snowboard in designated ski areas and do not cross boundaries into unsafe terrain. Obey all the rules of snowboard parks.

- Skateboarders should stay clear of motor vehicle vehicle and pedestrian traffic. Snowboarders should observe all the etiquette of the ski hill and watch for slower, smaller skiers or snowboarders.

- In both sports, do not allow children to attempt more advanced maneuvers until they have mastered the basic skills. They should work on control instead of speed and they should stop boarding when they become fatigued.

- Riders should check their boards before use for broken or loose parts.

- There should be proper lighting if you are skateboarding or snowboarding at night.

3. Skis, Toboggans, and Sleds

Sliding down a snow-covered hill is a lot of fun for children and adults alike. This can be a great outdoor activity for the whole family. But without proper safety practices, injuries can happen. As a paramedic I have attended too many tobogganing injuries; those injuries have been as serious as severe head injuries and broken backs. Tobogganing is fun, but teach your children to do it safely.

Skiing, tobogganing, and sledding are all subject to the prevailing weather conditions. Commercial ski areas often post the conditions so that skiers can use appropriate equipment. Traditionally, family tobogganing, sledding, and some skiing takes place in less formal settings on local, unregulated hills. Safety standards often rest in good judgment and experience. Here are some tips to keep your snow fun safe:

Helmets will reduce the chance of a head injury in skiing, tobogganing, or sledding. Ski helmets have not been standardized in Canada; however, we can rely on the European standards for them. There is no approved tobogganing helmet, but it is known that a hockey helmet is not adequate; a bicycling helmet is more appropriate because it protects against one major blow — after which it must be replaced.

In 1991, an ambulance was called to a popular sledding hill. The hill was very icy at the time and conditions allowed sleds to travel farther than they normally would. A young girl went down the hill, hit a building which was at the bottom of the hill and received a severe head injury. Though she survived, she spent many months in rehabilitation. Looking back at the situation and thinking of the circumstances, I probably would not have hesitated to slide down the hill with my daughter. That incident opened my eyes to how deceptive conditions can be on sledding hills.

While this book was being written, a four year-old boy was killed after his toboggan crashed into a tree. Between 179 to 189 tobogganing-related injuries were treated at Alberta Children's Hospital alone between March 1990 and February 1995. Half of those were head injuries, and the injuries included some severe cases of brain damage. Compared to tobogganing head injuries, the figures for head injuries in skiing, bicycling, and hockey are four or five times greater (Calgary Herald, Feb. 5, 1995, p. A3).

- Ensure children are dressed for winter conditions. Carefully consider wind chill factors, ice, snow melt, and slushy pools at the bottom of the hill. Will your child be warm and dry after a few runs down the hill? Don't forget appropriate eye protection and sunscreen.

- Inspect the area where the child will be sledding or skiing. Make sure the path is clear of rocks, trees, poles, and other obstacles.

Check it Out

- The sledding surface should be snow-packed and not icy. Ice contributes to speed and increases hazards.

- The ski surface should be completely covered with snow, relatively soft and free of obstacles that could cause injuries.

- Do not allow the children to ski or sled where they will run out onto the road. Fatalities have happened in this way.

- Make sure the sled is in good condition with no broken parts. Don't use a sled with splinters or protruding hardware. Skis, bindings, boots, and poles should be in good condition.

- When sledding or tobogganing, riding in a prone position can increase the chance of head and abdominal injury; therefore, the child's head should be at the back of the sled and covered with a helmet. Sitting is a better position.

- Teach children how to stop when sliding down snowy hills. "Snow-plowing" or merely falling to the hillside will stop most skiers. Sleds frequently have a breaking mechanism, though toboggans do not. Always keep in mind that toboggans can be highly uncontrollable devices.

- Make sure children know the difference between going down a hill fast and going down a hill out of control. Speed can kill.

- Instruct children to wait their turn and do not go until their path is clear of other children, parents, and dogs. Have them walk up the hill to the side, far from the path of the people sledding or skiing down.

- Skiers should stay well separated from people on toboggans or sleds.

4. Boats and Water Safety

Most children enjoy being in or near water. Unfortunately, they seldom consider the potential dangers. You have seen in Chapters Three and Thirteen that where there is water, there are hazards for children that can result in drowning.

The recreational use of boats is steadily increasing in North America and every year there are too many tragic stories of children drowning while being around boats and docks. Water safety on lakes, rivers, and sea environments is critical. Even small children can be taught some of the fundamentals of water safety and there are excellent courses for both you and your child. There are some fundamental water safety tips for being around boats, water and docks. Practice them — children will also learn by your example.

- Enroll your child in a swimming course. This is a good place for children to learn about water safety.

- Supervise children in boats, on docks, and on beaches. Don't let them out of your sight for even a moment. Ensure that there is an appropriate ratio of adults to children when you are supervising boating or beach fun.

- Life jackets must be worn in the boat and on all docks. Make sure your life jacket and your child's is properly adjusted worn correctly according to manufacturer's directions, and that all zippers and belts are fastened at all times.

- Make sure your life jackets (or personal floatation devices) are appropriate for your height and weight and that they are approved by the Department of Transport.

- Inflatable beach toys and air mattresses are no substitute for personal floatation devices and are not intended for that use.

- Avoid running and horseplay on docks. Docks are usually slippery, hard, and frequently have equipment and ropes on them.

- Diving off a dock is dangerous. Shallow water, rocks, and other obstructions may cause the sudden and violent impact to the head that results in tragic spinal cord injuries or even death.

- Wear appropriate footwear when boating and especially on wooden docks that are prone to splintered wood. Snug-fitting shoes without heels and with non-skid soles are excellent choices. Certain shoes that are designed for both children and adults, are designed to be worn from the beach right into the water, protecting delicate feet from sharp stones.

- Make sure that your motor boat has appropriate emergency equipment on board sufficient for the number of passengers it can carry: extra life jackets, oars, a bailer, flares, blankets, extra ropes, flotation device(s), fire extinguisher, and a first aid kit.

- Run a tight ship! In the limited spaces of a water craft, gear and tools must be stored safely and neatly. The captain of the ship assumes the responsibility for all passengers, and therefore, authority rests with the captain.

- When fueling — everybody out of the boat! That's not only prudent, but it's the law in most provinces and states.

- For extended boating trips, tell someone where you are going and when you intend to return. Check all fuel, safety equipment, and supplies to ensure you are equipped for all possible eventualities.

- Check the extended maritime forecast and tide charts for the territory you plan to cover. Remember that weather conditions on or near water can change rapidly.

5. All-Terrain Vehicles and Snowmobiles

All-terrain Vehicles (ATVs) and snowmobiles have become very popular recreation vehicles. Safety-minded parents who normally would not let children operate comparable farm machinery or motorcycles are letting young children operate these vehicles. If children are not themselves operating the ATVs or snowmobile, they may be passengers on one. Again, supervision, safe equipment, and proper training are the keys to safety in using ATVs and snowmobiles. Here are some considerations for their use:

- Helmets reduce the chance of a head injury in both sports and have prevented many serious injuries and fatalities. Make sure you have an approved helmet for each rider and that they are worn.

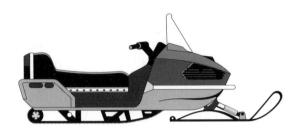

- Ensure children are appropriately dressed for the weather conditions. Carefully consider the weather, the terrain, and the length of time you will be travelling on the vehicle.

- Instruct your children in the safe use of all-terrain vehicles and snowmobiles. ATVs, especially the three-wheeled models, may be very unstable. Careless operation of snowmobiles is often the cause of serious injuries and fatalities.

- Make sure that all operators, of any age, of ATVs and snowmobiles have been given a thorough safety orientation that includes an orientation to the terrain.

- If you plan an extended trip on an ATV or a snowmobile, let someone know where you are going and the expected duration of your trip.

- Ensure that lengthy trail rides are taken on vehicles equipped with emergency supplies such as survival gear, matches, flashlights, extra clothing, and a first aid kit.

Motor Vehicle Safety

17

Your child will no doubt be spending more time in your motor vehicle and there are certain safety standards you should be aware of. I will cover some of the steps you can take to prevent many dangers that could lead to serious injury.

The leading cause of death in preschool and school-aged children is motor vehicle collisions. This is true of pedestrians, cyclists, and passengers. Motor vehicle collisions account for 20% of injury deaths to children under one year of age. From 1986 to 1990 in Canada, over 424 preschoolers died as a result of motor vehicle injuries: 45% of those deaths occurred when they were passengers, and 45% occurred when they were pedestrians. (Canadian Institute of Child Health, 1994:23, 45-6, 63-4).

1. General Motor Vehicle Safety Tips for Children

It is hard to imagine a cargo more precious than a child. When a child becomes a passenger in your vehicle, there is a whole set of considerations that must be your conscious responsibility. In that situation, it is not only your life you are dealing with. Here are a few general tips for motor vehicle safety from the Safe Journey brochure produced by Canadian Living Magazine:

- First and foremost, make sure your vehicle is in good repair. Don't forget the small, obvious parts. For example, door locks should be in good working order and childproof. Examine your vehicle's exhaust system and make sure it is in good order.

- From the moment you get into your car, motor vehicle safety should be a major consideration. There have been too many incidents where children have been run over in the driveways of their own homes. Always circle your vehicle before you drive away to ensure your path is clear.

- Children must learn from an early age that when they are in the car, they must be buckled up. Set a good example by having every adult also buckle up before the vehicle moves.

- Reduce internal distractions. Ask passengers to keep noise to a minimum and to remain seat-belted at all times.

- No lollipops, popsicles, or hard candies in the car. If you have to come to a sudden stop, they could lodge in your child's throat and cause a choking problem.

- Make it a rule that only selected toys are allowed in the car. Avoid sharp-edged, hard, or heavy toys that could become dangerous UFOs in the event of a sudden stop.

- Make sure little fingers stay away from car doors. Ask "All hands clear?" before closing a vehicle door. Keep fingers far from the door by asking young children to give themselves a hug while you close the door.

- All doors remain locked while children are in the car. Children should be told to keep their hands off the locks and door and window handles (or window buttons), and not to lean against the door.

- All body parts remain inside the car. The windows in a moving car should not be allowed to be lowered more than half-way.

- If a fight or a disturbance starts, the driver should pull over and stop. It is difficult to drive with a back seat battle going on. Providing children with toys and games to keep curious hands occupied helps to enforce order in a positive way.

Our rescue department was called to a shopping mall in December, 1994 for a possible carbon monoxide poisoning. When I arrived a mother was frantic because her three young children were locked in her car which was left running while she went into the grocery store. She had also locked the keys in the car. The children did not wake up with yelling through the windows and pounding on the car. My response was to break a window and open the doors. The children were taken in an ambulance to the hospital for suspected carbon monoxide poisoning. Fortunately, the emergency physician determined that they had not been poisoned, but were just heavy sleepers.

- Never leave your child unattended in a car; never leave the vehicle with keys in the ignition. Toddlers and young children learn by imitating adults. How many times has your child watched your drive? Children have been known to start vehicles, put them in gear and, quite literally, go for a spin. There have been several cases where motor vehicles have been stolen with children inside.

- The temperature of a vehicle's interior may reach excessive levels when it is parked in the sun. Children have become very ill when they were left in a hot vehicle. Dehydration, heat stroke, and even death can occur in a surprisingly short period of time when small children and infants are exposed to excessive heat conditions.

- The surfaces of a child's car seat that has been left in the direct rays of the sun can reach temperatures that can burn a child's skin. Try to park your vehicle in the shade, or cover the seat with a towel or jacket to prevent it from heating up. If you're not sure whether the seat has been heated in your absence, touch the seat with the back side of your hand to test its temperature before putting the child into it.

- Window shades or screens that attach to a vehicle window can shade the child from direct sunlight. Another product is a polarized film that sticks to the inside of the window and acts as a filtering sunscreen much the way sunglasses do. Remember, do not use anything that will block your view.

2. Motor Vehicle Child Seats and Safety

One of the first things you will be doing as a new parent is taking your child from the hospital to your home in your vehicle. It is tempting to hold the infant in your arms, expecting that in a collision your seat belt will protect you both. This is a tragic error. In a crash in which the car is travelling only 30 mph (50 kph), a 10 pound (4.5 kg.) infant will be ripped from a belted adult's arm with a force of almost 200 pounds (91 kg.). The child's body becomes a projectile travelling with such force that it can fly into the dashboard or even smash through the windshield.

During a collision, a child in an adult's lap is thrown from the adult's arms.
Information reproduced with permission from "Keep Them Safe", Transport Canada

Kids for Keeps

*In a two-vehicle collision, a semi-conscious woman kept ask-
ing for her "baby." Her vehicle had sustained heavy damage
and was thoroughly searched. No baby or car seat was was
in sight, although diapers, baby bottles and toys were found
in the back seat. A search of the surrounding area revealed the
unconscious child, still buckled into the car seat. The car seat
was not secured into the vehicle at the time of the accident.
The child sustained severe head injuries but lived.*

Infant carriers, car seats, booster seats, and the correct use of
seat belts can save the life of your child. The special protection
of a correctly installed and used infant safety seat cannot be
stressed enough. Whether it is a short trip down the block or a
long vacation trip, these seats must be used. Here are some general pointers for their use:

- The safest child seats are the ones that will be used correctly every time. Misuse of child seats can partially or
  even completely nullify their benefit. Correctly installed
  and used, child seats are extremely effective, reducing
  the risk of death by 71%, hospitalization by 67%, and
  minor injuries by 50% (Alberta Coalition on Child Passenger Restraint).

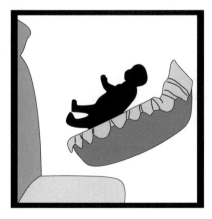

Devices that do not meet Motor Vehicle Safety Standards (such as this car bed) do not
provide protection for a child during an accident or sudden stop. Information
reproduced with permission from "Keep Them Safe", Transport Canada

- It is imperative that you follow manufacturer's directions when using any child restraint device.

- Read and follow manufacturer's instructions closely. If you do not understand the instructions, seek assistance. If you are unsure of the requirements for car seats, contact Transport Canada, the local Traffic Safety Board, or the Canadian Motor Association.

- Ensure that car seats meet Canadian standards. Manufacturers of child restraints must indicate compliance on a label affixed to the seat stating that it meets the Canadian Motor Vehicle Safety Standard (CMVSS) 213.1, 213 or 213.2 for infant carriers, child seats, and booster cushions, respectively. The label must also state the size of a child for which the seat is designed and instructions must be provided on how it is to be installed ("Keep Them Safe," Transport Canada).

- Car seats purchased outside of Canada may not meet these standards. Children's car seats used in the U.S.A. do not require the use of tether straps. Using a seat without a tether strap in Canada is illegal.

Buckle Up Right

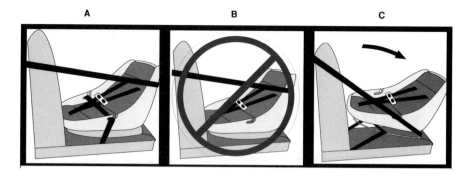

All child restraint systems must be properly installed, according to the manufacturer's instructions. If this is not done, the product may fail, as shown here. Figure A shows the correct installation of a rear-facing infant carrier. Figure B shows an incorrect installation. Figure C shows an incorrectly installed seat during an automobile collision. Information reproduced with permission from "Keep Them Safe", Transport Canada

3. The Infant Carrier

The infant carrier is designed for children from birth to 20 pounds (9 kg.). The infant is secured in the carrier by a harness system. The carrier is attached to the vehicle by the seat belt. These carriers must be secured facing the rear of the vehicle, preferably in the center of the rear seat. The rear seat is safer because it is farther away from the windshield and the steering wheel. But if you are travelling by yourself, and feel you must have the infant beside you in the front seat, secure the carrier facing the rear of the vehicle. Baby supply shops market a rear view mirror to attach to your existing rear view mirror that will allow you to check on your baby without having to turn around and take your attention off the road.

Babies are less likely to feel car sick than older children. Many will probably fall asleep in a safety seat and, as every parent knows, a calm child means a calm driver — and a safer trip. Here are some tips to make your infant's ride more comfortable:

- In accordance with the vehicle manufacturer's recommendations, Transport Canada recommends that all infant carriers be placed in the center of the back seat rather than the front seat. If you are travelling alone with the baby, you may wish to secure the rear-facing infant carrier in the front passenger seat. This allows you to check on the child without taking your attention off driving.

- In newer vehicles, air bags in the front passenger seat may cause the infant injury if they are activated.

- Many infant seats have more than one reclining position. Check the manufacturer's instructions to make sure you're using the correct position.

- "Head-huggers" are commercially made pads that fit into the car seat to support the child's head and body. Rolled diapers or blankets will do the same job.

- In cold weather, cut holes in a blanket and pull the straps through, or wrap the blanket around the baby *after doing up the harness.*

- Make sure the baby's back is flat against the car seat. If the back is curved the baby may be uncomfortable.

- Be aware of the sun shining through back windows onto your child.

- Some infant seats can also be moved in and out of the car and can double as baby seats in the house.

- Never leave a child unsupervised in an infant carrier.

- Always follow manufacturer's direction for installation.

4. Combination Seats

A combination car seat can be used for the infant as a rear-facing carrier and, when the child is older, as a front-facing car seat. Although 9 kg (20 lbs.) was generally considered the weight at which an infant could be placed in a forward-facing child restraint, the child's physical development is considered more crucial in defining when to place an infant forward facing. For example, there are infants who are 9 kg (20 lbs.) but only 4 or 5 months old. The neck muscles of these infants are not strong enough to support the weight of their head, and the seat should therefore be left in a rear-facing position. Once infants can sit up unaided for long periods of time without falling over, or can pull themselves up to a standing position, it is safe to place the seat in a forward-facing position.

Infants: *Birth to 9 kg (20 lbs.)*
                 Rear-facing Position

When the combination seat is used for an infant, the seat faces the rear of the vehicle and the baby is held in the child car seat by the harness system. The seat is secured by the vehicle seat belt system.

Be sure to adjust all harness straps properly to secure the baby safely and comfortably. Always follow the manufacturer's instructions.

Toddlers: *9 kg (20 lbs.) to 22 kg (48 lbs.)*
                 Forward-facing Position

The child is secured in the car seat by the shoulder harness. In addition, the seats have a retaining device such as an abdominal shield, "T" shield, arm bar, 3-point harness, 5-point harness, or a combination of these. These devices help to distribute the forces of impact over the strongest parts of the child's body. Tests show that all these different types of restraining devices provide the same level of protection when used properly.

Combination Seat

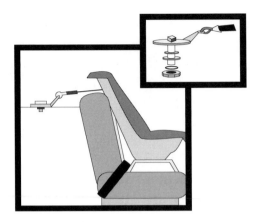

Tether straps are provided with child car seats to help keep the top of the seat in place during a collision or sudden stop. The strap must be attached to a bolt anchored to the vehicle. Information reproduced with permission from "Keep Them Safe", Transport Canada

Transport Canada's safety regulations state that the maximum distance a child's head can move forward during a crash at 50 km/h (30 mph) is 720 mm (28.4 in.). (Less than five percent of actual frontal collisions are more severe than this crash test.) Currently, this regulation can only be met if the child seat is held in place by the vehicle seat belt system and by a tether strap. The tether strap prevents the top of the seat from moving forward in a collision or sudden stop.

If a tether strap is not used, the child car seat moves forward in a collision, causing the child's head to move dangerously forward. Information reproduced with permission from "Keep Them Safe", Transport Canada

Kids for Keeps

The tether strap must be securely attached to a bolt anchored to the rear shelf of a car or the floor of a van, station wagon, or hatchback.

Passenger cars (with the exception of convertibles) manufactured after January 1,1989 have built-in tether anchorage locations. For vehicles manufactured prior to 1989 (or vehicles other than passenger cars, such as pickup trucks, passenger vans, and so on), contact a dealership of your vehicle manufacturer. Most manufacturers have information on proper anchoring of tether straps. If you have difficulty obtaining this information from a dealer, contact your local CAA office for assistance.

5. Booster Cushions

For children over 18 kg (40 lbs.)

A booster cushion may be used for:

- children who are too tall for their car seat (when the mid-point of the child's ears is above the child car seat), or
- children over 18 kg (40 lbs.)

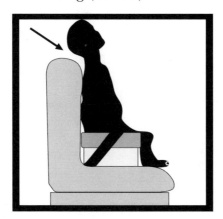

If a child's head protrudes over the vehicle seat back, it will snap back in a collision, causing serious injury. In this case, no booster cushion should be used. Information reproduced with permission from "Keep Them Safe", Transport Canada

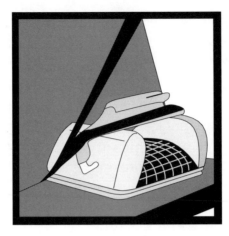

Booster cushions, like all other child restraint systems, must be correctly installed. Information reproduced with permission from "Keep Them Safe", Transport Canada

In vehicles with a low seat back, the child's head may protrude over the vehicle seat back when placed in a booster cushion. In this case, the child must be placed in the vehicle seat belt system

Booster Cushion

without the use of a booster cushion. The lap belt must be placed low on the hips.

6. Integrated (Built-in) Child Seats

Some vehicles have child restraint systems built into the vehicle seat bench. These seats are required to meet *CMVSS 213.4*. Since these seats are built right into the vehicle seat bench, they do not require the use of a tether strap. At the time of printing, two types of integrated seats were available:

- forward-facing seats for toddlers who are one year or older and who weigh 9 kg (20 lbs.) to 22 kg (48 lbs.), and

- booster seats for children over 18 kg (40 lbs.).

7.

ATTENTION

W Since the printing of this book, new   kg (20
lb recommendations from Transport Canada include: lless of
wl   its vary
ar **Do not place a rear-facing infant carrier or toddler** etween
9   **seat in a passenger seat equipped with an airbag.** parents
or **Infants and children under age 12 should sit in the** nd taxi
di   **back seat. The centre seat is the safest.**   a child
ca **If you must transport children age 12 and under in** ailable,
tl   **the front passenger seat, consider deactivating the** ored by
tl   **airbag. Contact Transport Canada and your**   ole, the
cl   **automobile dealer on how to do this.**   nsuring

that the lap portion of the seat belt is as low on the hips as possible, and that it is snug across the chest.

8. Protecting the Unborn Child

The best way to protect an unborn child in a motor vehicle collision is to protect the mother. Pregnant women should always wear the lap and shoulder belt when riding in a vehicle. The belt should be worn low over the pelvic bones and not against the soft stomach area. It should be as snug as possible without being uncomfortable.

9. Protecting Older Children

Children who have outgrown a booster cushion must wear a seat belt. Ensure that the lap belt is worn low and snug over the lap area, not over the stomach. *Never place the shoulder strap under the arm. This can cause serious internal injuries in a vehicle collision.*

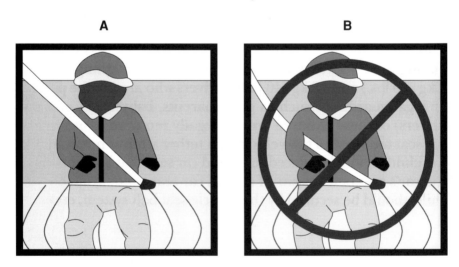

Figure A shows the correct positioning of the seat belt. Figure B shows an incorrect positioning of the seat belt. The shoulder belt must be placed across the the chest, and the lap belt worn low and snug over the lap area. Information reproduced with permission from "Keep Them Safe", Transport Canada

Kids for Keeps

10. Shopping for a Child Restraint System

A. When Shopping for a Child Restraint System, Ensure that:

- The seat is appropriate for the height, weight and muscular development of your child and that the seat allows space for the child to grow.

- It can be installed correctly in your vehicle. This means trying the seat in your vehicle to ensure that at least 85 percent of the base of the child restraint is supported by the vehicle seat, and ensuring your vehicle seat belt will fit through or around the restraint in the manner recommended by the manufacturer.

- It has been bought in Canada and bears a *Statement of Compliance* label certifying that it meets Canadian safety standards. Seats bought in other countries, including the United States, are not likely to meet strict Canadian standards.

- The child is comfortable in the seat.

- You have proper instructions on its use.

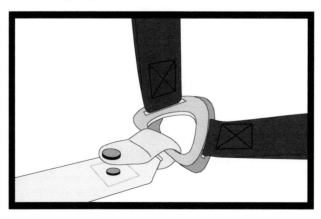

The "Waterbury Buckle". Information reproduced with permission from "Keep Them Safe", Transport Canada

B. Used Child Restraint Systems

While child restraint systems manufactured prior to 1982 met the applicable safety standards at the time of their manufacture, they should be avoided. Some of the problems with used restraint systems are:

- missing instructions, which increases the possibility of misuse

- wear-and-tear on the harness, plastic shell and pad, which results in decreased performance

- the "Waterbury Buckle" (a horseshoe-shaped clasp with a dome button (snap) found on older units can be easily undone by children.

Although older child restraints may provide a high level of protection if they are properly used, there are often parts and instructions missing, making the chance of misuse very high.

11. Special Case Installations

A. Vehicles with Automatic Restraint Systems

More and more vehicles are being equipped with automatic lap/shoulder belt systems, where the end of the belt is attached to the inside of car door. As the door opens, the belt stretches with the door, allowing the occupant to get in and out. As the door closes, the belt automatically wraps around the passenger. Child restraints cannot be used with automatic seat belt systems because the lap portion of the seat belt does not hold the restraint firmly in place. In cases where child seats must be used in a seating position with automatic seat belts, a floor-mounted (manual) belt, available from the vehicle dealer must be installed. (All vehicles with automatic seat belts are required to have an anchorage point on the floor that can be used to attach a manual seat belt.) For more information, consult your vehicle owner's manual, or see your dealer.

B. Vehicles with Continuous Loop Lap/Shoulder Belts

Some vehicles have continuous loop lap/shoulder belts with metal tongues that slide freely up and down the belt. These seat belt systems have an emergency locking retractor designed to allow freedom of movement during regular driving and to lock up during hard-braking or impact. The problem is that when used with child restraints the lap belt can work loose as the car swerves and turns corners. With continuous loop lap/shoulder belts, a locking clip must be used to prevent the lap portion of the belt from loosening. This device is a special H-shaped metal clip that locks together the lap and shoulder portion of the seat belt, keeping the child car seat firmly in place.

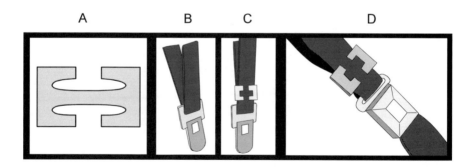

The locking clip (A) holds the metal tongue in place in vehicles with continuous loop lap / shoulder belts. (B) shows a continuous loop belt without the locking clip in place. (C) shows the locking clip installed. (D) shows the locking clip in place when the lap seat is buckled up. Information reproduced with permission from "Keep Them Safe", Transport Canada

Bicycle Safety

18

C ycling seems to be enjoying a tremendous revival with the advent of advanced technologies in equipment design, materials, and construction. Cycling trails are being created in all kinds of settings, from urban centers to wilderness parks. If you enjoy cycling you might want to take your child cycling with you.

Some infants accompany the cyclist safely tucked into a specially designed tandem trailer for infants and small children. When the child is old enough to sit up by herself, and has neck muscles strong enough to hold her head with a helmet on, the child may be ready for riding in a child carrier on your bike. No child under the age of one year should be transported in a child carrier. Eventually your children will be old enough and mature enough to ride beside you on their own bikes. Cycling safety is essential for every stage of your child's bicycle experience.

Safe cyclists know the rules of the road. Cyclists should not ride on sidewalks but on the street where they must follow the same laws as motorists. Training to improve your cycling skills in traffic is available in many communities. Contact your provincial or state cycling association, the local cycling club or the local safety council for programs offered in your community.

The primary safety rule for bicycling is the wearing of an appropriate and properly fitting helmet. Before discussing child carriers for bicycles and youth bicycles, I have included a section on bicycle helmets.

1. Cycling Helmets

Bicycling and many other sports such as skiing, hockey, skateboarding, and rollerblading are responsible for many deaths and serious injuries. However, bicycle accidents cause the most common head injuries in children.

The statistics are frightening — and clear.

Last year, almost 100 children in Canada died from head injuries caused by falling off their bicycles. Thousands more were injured, some with permanent disabilities. In the U.S.A., the Center for Disease Control estimates that if all bicyclists wore helmets, perhaps 500 lives and 135,000 head injuries could be prevented each year; that is, there would be at least a 50% reduction in cycling-related head injuries.

Less than 20% of reported cycling injuries involved collisions with motor vehicles; most injuries occur in falls or as a result of riders losing control. Bicycle riders who wear helmets are eight times less likely to incur serious brain injuries than riders who do not wear helmets (Canadian Dental Association pamphlet, "Protect Your Family from Head Injury").

Here are some tips about bicycle helmets:

- Make sure your child wears a helmet when bicycling. Bicycle helmets save lives and years of rehabilitation. Train your child from the start that you are not uncool or "nerdy" if you wear a helmet.

- When picking a helmet, make sure it has an approval seal from the Canadian Standards Association (CSA) or the private Snell Memorial Foundation. In the U.S.A., it should have a Snell seal, or American National Standard Institute (ANSI) label.

- A helmet should have a hard plastic outer shell with an energy-absorbing liner.

- The helmet should fit snugly so it will not slide around on the child's head.

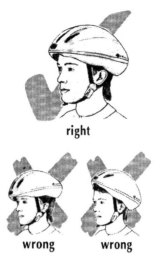

right

wrong   wrong

Bicycle Helmets
(Information courtesy of the Edmonton Grey Nuns Bicycle Helmet Campaign and the Edmonton Board of Health)

- Many helmets will come with an assortment of foam shims which can be placed inside the helmet to ensure it fits smaller heads. Follow the manufacturer's directions for the proper fitting of these pads.

- A helmet should also have an adjustable chin strap with a quick release fastener.

- Make sure the helmet is lightweight, comfortable, and is well-ventilated.

- If a helmet has been involved in a serious fall, replace it at once.

- Don't store your helmet away from your bike — attach it to your bicycle so that it's always ready to wear.

Ideally, when you are purchasing a helmet, you should take your child with you to make sure that it fits properly. For a proper fit, carefully measure the circumference of the head about 1 inch (3cm) above the eyebrows. If you are unsure about making this measurement, ask your doctor or a public health nurse to assist you.

A helmet that fits properly has these features:

- It is level from the front to the back and sits about 1 inch (3 cm) above the eyebrows.

- The helmet sits squarely on top of the head, protecting the forehead and the base of the skull (back of the head).

- It fits snugly, but not too tightly; it should neither slide around on the child's head, nor pinch.

- The helmet has straps that are tight and comfortable.

- It cannot be "rolled" forward or backward and can only be removed by undoing the straps.

2. Child Carriers on Bicycles

Many adults who enjoy cycling will be eager to share the experience with their young child. Child carriers are widely used on the back of adult bicycles. However, because the carrier changes the load distribution of the bike, which in turn affects the steering and braking, the Canadian Pediatric Society considers them dangerous and does not recommend their use.

Children in carriers have been seriously injured when the bicycle they were riding on tipped over. The child is very vulnerable when this happens. If you are not an experienced rider and have not practiced with extra weight on the carrier on the bike, don't go for the ride with your child.

If you do decide to use a child carrier on your bike, please follow these rules:

- Ensure you can handle a bicycle with the extra weight of a child on the back of the bike. Practice with a similar weight load before taking your child on the bicycle. Use a bag of sand, for instance, to see how the bike handles with the extra weight. Make sure the manufacturer's recommended load is not exceeded.

- Choose a seat with safety straps that cannot be undone by the child and that will prevent the child from making unexpected moves.

- The carrier should be solid, rigid, and fastened securely to the bicycle frame according to the manufacturer's instructions. Check to see that it is secure every time you go for a ride.

- The carrier should be designed to prevent the child's feet and hands from getting caught in the spokes.

- The seat should have a high back to support the child's head and neck, and side supports to prevent a child from swinging from side to side.

- Dress the child properly. Remember that, unlike you, the child will not be exerting himself. You may be warm and sweaty while the child is cold.

- If the seat on your bicycle has springs, use a guard that will prevent little fingers from getting caught.

Keep Your Head

- Both the child and the adult should wear approved helmets that are properly fastened.

- Do not ride on busy streets and always ride with extreme caution.

- Do not lean the bicycle against anything or use a kickstand when your child is in the seat.

3. Children's Bicycles

Before children are old enough to ride a bike by themselves, they probably know from first-hand experience that bikes are a good means of exercise and a lot of fun. Sooner or later your children will want a bike of their own.

Parents should remember is that there are approximately 50,000 Canadian children injured each year while riding their bicycles. Of these, 70-100 children die from their injuries each year. Head injuries take the greatest toll, with bike crashes being the leading cause of head injury in school age children (Calgary Herald, Feb. 5, 1995, p. A3).

When your child is physically big enough and old enough to understand the hazards of bicycle riding, you may want to follow these tips:

- Make sure he or she always wear an approved helmet. (Set a good example and always wear yours.)

- The bike should be the proper size. A guideline for sizing is that when your child sits on the seat with her hands on the handlebars the balls of her feet should be able to reach the floor.

- If the bike has a center bar, your child should be able to straddle the bar with both feet flat on the floor. There should be about two inches clearance between the bar and his crotch.

- Teach children that a bike is not a toy and they must ride in a responsible manner.

- Your child must know how to steer the bike and how to use the brakes on the bicycle. If your child cannot stop the bike by using the brakes, she is not ready to ride it on the street. Practice these skills on wide, flat surfaces, away from pedestrians and other vehicles until your child has perfected appropriate techniques.

- Instruct children in the rules of the road. Your children should always ride with a responsible adult until they have the skills, the knowledge, and the maturity to handle the bike on their own.

- Before children can go bicycling on their own, they should know and be prepared to obey all traffic signs. They should know how to signal when they are turning, and know enough to exercise caution when riding close to parked motor vehicles.

Toy Safety — 19

Most parents and grandparents enjoy buying toys for children. However, some toys can be more hazardous than fun. Caution should be taken when buying toys or receiving toys for your child from friends and relatives. A toy that is a lot of fun for a five year-old can become very dangerous in the hands of a one year-old.

A major danger to infants and small children when they are playing with toys is choking. Small toys or parts of toys can break off and end up in a child's mouth, creating a choking hazard. When purchased, toys should have an age recommendation on the packaging, though you should never assume this to be 100% accurate for all children. In Canada there is a report produced by the Canadian Toy Testing Council that is published every year in the fall. The Toy Report is a useful volume that covers toys for children aged newborn to ten years old. It is available at large magazine stands and you should be able to find a copy of it at the library.

1. General Tips for Toy Safety

- Before you buy the toy, or accept it as a gift, remember to check it for potential dangers. Toys should be washable, have smooth edges, have no removable pins or buttons, and have no springs to catch fingers, toes or hair.

- Inspect your child's toys regularly for wear or damage.

- Do not try to "challenge" your child with toys that are designed for older children. Toys can be dangerous if not age-appropriate. Think about whether a younger child in the house may have access to the toy. Older children can be taught to keep their toys where younger siblings cannot reach them.

- Supervise your child's play. Young children, especially, have not yet learned how to play well together and can easily hurt each other.

- Show your children how to use the toys properly. Teach them to watch for danger in toys and to let you know if something is broken or hazardous. Teach your child that some toys can be unsafe.

- Watch for broken or cracked rattles. Many rattles contain beads which can be easily swallowed or aspirated (inhaled) into a lung.

- Use the toy gauge, available from Consumer and Corporate Affairs Canada, to check that your baby's toys are large enough that they will not cause choking. (See Chapter Three, Choking, Suffocation, Strangulation and Drowning for additional information about choking and strangulation dangers with toys.)

- Make sure your infant cannot reach the mobile in the playpen or crib. By four to five months your child will grab hold of anything in reach. Once he can roll over and push himself up, it is time to remove mobiles. Mobiles pose a strangulation hazard if the child can reach them and pull them down.

- When a baby can stand, remove all toys from the crib that could entangle clothing and cause strangulation.

One toy I came across was a stuffed dog with a hard plastic nose. The nose was attached to the dog by a sharp serrated piece of metal which was easily pulled out.

- Avoid toys with buttons or removable eyes and noses that may pose a choking hazard.

- Remove ribbons from stuffed animals. A baby may pull a ribbon off and put it into his mouth and choke on it.

- Balloons are not toys! Keep children from sucking or chewing on inflated or uninflated balloons. Keep uninflated balloons away from children. Get rid of broken balloons at once; make sure you have all the pieces of a broken balloon. Adults should inflate balloons for children rather than allowing the child to do it.

- Foam toys can be dangerous if pieces are torn and the foam is put into little mouths. Be especially vigilant with stuffed toys; they can develop tears or ripped seams which will expose the stuffing.

- Caution is needed with second-hand toys; they may not meet safety standards. For instance, old toys could be painted with lead-based paint, which would be a hazard. (See Chapter Four, *Poisoning.*)

- Keep batteries away from children. Small button-type batteries that are found in some toys, calculators, and watches have been swallowed or choked on by children.

- Toys that shoot, especially those using darts or arrows, should never be pointed at another child, adult, or pet. Many injuries have been caused by these toys. Children should be discouraged from playing with them.

- Teach children to put toys away after use. Toyboxes without a lid or ones that have sliding doors or panels are the safest. If your toybox does have a lid, make sure that it has holes in two or more adjacent sides to prevent suffocation of a child who may become trapped inside.

- Toys left on the floor or stairs are a danger to children and adults alike (see Chapter Two, *Falls*).

2. Tricycles and Other Toddler Riding Toys

Once a child has mastered a tricycle or a riding toy, they are very mobile, they can move very rapidly, and injuries can happen very quickly. Riding toys are fun; make them safe fun.

- A helmet reduces the chance of a head injury. Remember that helmets must be worn when using all riding toys.

- Stability is important. The wheels of tricycles and riding toys should be spaced wide enough apart to keep the toy stable.

- Extreme caution is needed when driving in or out of the driveway. Many children have been killed when someone has driven over them. Remember, children are small and hard to see when you are in the driver's seat! Walk around the vehicle before you get into your motor vehicle, and then proceed with caution.

- Do not allow your child on a riding toy anywhere close to the stairs.

- Many fatalities have resulted when a child on a riding toy has rolled into the street. Keep children on riding toys off sloping driveways and off of the street.

- Many riding toys are very low to the ground and very difficult to see. A flag on a tall flexible pole attached to the riding toy might make it a little bit more visible.

3. Hand-crafted Toys and Gifts

Hand-crafted toys and gifts are fun to receive, but they must also be safe. Because of their uniqueness and because they are usually made by local craftspersons, they are not covered in the Canadian Toy Testing Council's report. As a parent, you must rely on the sensibilities and knowledge of the toy maker, and your own awareness of what makes a safe toy. Manufacturers and vendors of hand-crafted toys are responsible for ensuring that these items are safe and meet the requirements of the Hazardous Products Act.

The Hazardous Products Act and Regulations are intended to reduce hidden dangers to consumers. Of special concern are mechanical hazards which could physically injure a child; chemical hazards which could result in poisoning or injury if materials are ingested or in contact with skin; and flammability hazards associated with the materials used to make the toy or gift. Whether you are a craftsperson making one special item for a child in your family, or are producing toys and gifts for the marketplace, *make them safe*.

When you are purchasing, or when you are designing and crafting toys, keep these points in mind:

- Toys intended for use by children under three years of age should not contain separable parts or small pieces which could pose a choking hazard. Buttons, ornamentation, or other small pieces must be securely attached.

- Stuffing material must be non-toxic, clean, and free of hard or foreign matter. Beans or plant seeds are not permitted. Manufacturers or importers of upholstered or stuffed articles should check with the provincial Consumer Affairs office for more information on the Upholstered and Stuffed Articles Act.

- Wooden toys must have a smooth finish to prevent slivers.

- Toys should not have sharp edges or sharp metal points which could harm children.

- All screws, nails, staples, and other fasteners must be properly secured and countersunk or covered if necessary.

- Toy boxes with lids, a common craft item, should have holes in two or more adjacent sides to prevent the suffocation of any child who may become trapped inside.

- Play furniture should be firm and level.

- Push and pull toys with a shaft-like handle that is $\frac{3}{8}$ inches (.95 cm) in diameter or less should have a protective tip on the handle to prevent a puncture wound.

- Rattles should have all ends or protrusions large enough so that they will not easily fit into a child's throat. They should not contain plant seeds as a noise maker.

- Coatings such as paint or varnish must not contain lead, barium, or other toxic elements.

- Toys sold in plastic bags that are 14 inches (35.6 cm) or larger in circumference, require a warning to alert parents to the suffocation dangers associated with plastic bags. Remember, plastic bags are not toys and should never be given as a play thing to a child.

Holiday Safety   **20**

H olidays are a time for family and friends to get together, have fun and enjoy each other's company. It is also a time where injuries can happen at an alarming rate. Holidays often involve special decorations that can be potential fire hazards; the use of alcohol is sometimes increased; there are more people crowding into houses; and sometimes, less attention is paid to children because of visitors. Dangerous situations can happen quickly and without warning. With a bit of caution, you can have an injury-free holiday.

In this chapter, I focus primarily on Christmas, Hallowe'en and July 1st and 4th celebrations, though many of the concerns for these holidays may be extended to others.

1. Christmas without Hazards

During Christmas, many residential fires are attributed to cooking incidents, and many fires are caused by careless smoking. Fire is only one source of holiday tragedies. The danger of choking and poisoning increases at Christmas time because of the various ornaments, foods, wrapping paper, and ribbons that are found around the house. Reduce some of the common holiday hazards and have a safe and joyful celebration.

- Christmas trees can be a fire hazard. Until you put them up in your house, trees should be stored outdoors, preferably in the shade, until ready for use.

- The base of a natural Christmas tree should be in water. They need an incredible amount of water and will dry out quickly without a constant supply of water. Check your tree daily and take it down when it shows signs of drying out.

- Keep a No Smoking area around the Christmas tree and do not allow candles close to it. When a tree catches fire the flames spread at a horrifying rate. The tree should not block an exit.

- Make sure all Christmas lights are in good order. Do not use lights with frayed cords or loose connections. Use only cords, lights, and decorations that are approved by CSA (Canadian Standards Association) or Underwriters Limited (UL).

- The chance of a house fire increases with the extra cooking associated with the holidays. Pay attention to what you are doing in the kitchen. (See Chapter Six, *Burns and Scalds and Chapter Nine, The Kitchen.*)

- Children swallowing or biting Christmas light bulbs are a common problem at this time of year. Make sure that no ornaments are left lying around after they have fallen off the tree.

Christmas Treat?

Kids for Keeps

- Place ornaments high enough on the tree so that toddlers cannot reach them.

- Many of the plants used for decorations around the house at Christmas time are poisonous — such as the berries of the mistletoe. If you have a plant and are not sure whether it is poisonous, check with the Poison Control Center. (See Chapter Four, *Poisoning*)

- Keep batteries out of children's reach.

- Remember that peanuts, nuts, and hard candies can cause children to choke. Keep them out of the reach of children, especially children under five years of age.

- Wrapping paper and ribbons are objects that can potentially cause choking.

- Remember to keep balloons out of children's reach.

- Alcohol consumption increases in the holiday season. This affects your judgment not only when you are driving and cooking, but also when you are wrestling or playing with children.

2. Hallowe'en Safety

For most children, the end of October means Hallowe'en costumes, candy, and a good time. Costumes require special safety considerations and of course, trick-or-treating and its rewards should always be supervised by a responsible adult. Let's keep the little goblins safe!

- Your child's costume should be made from a flame-resistant material.

- Avoid baggy costumes that might cause the children to trip. Remember that in most areas they will be going up and down stairs all night.

- The costume should be visible. It will be dark and drivers will have a difficult time seeing little goblins. Reflective tape can be purchased at hardware or retail stores and applied to costumes and/or accessories.

- Masks can be very uncomfortable, but a bigger concern is that they will reduce a child's vision. Using non-toxic makeup and a bit of imagination will fix this problem by disguising your little one with face paint — besides, this will be more fun than a mask.

- Take your child trick-or-treating yourself or let them go with another responsible adult or a very responsible teenage sibling.

- Have the children stay on brightly lit streets where there are a lot of adults. It is not uncommon to hear of older bullies who will steal treats from smaller ones.

- Stay on the sidewalk and obey all pedestrian rules.

- We have all read in the papers about the horror of foreign objects such as pins and razor blades concealed in apples or other treats. Caution is always necessary — examine the goodies that your children receive before letting them eat them. Do not consume any unwrapped or opened treats.

3. Fireworks

National celebrations in Canada and in the U.S.A. often feature fireworks as a focal point of the festivities. Additionally, in many areas fireworks can be purchased all year round. Many severe injuries to adults as well as children are caused by fireworks every year.

One incident occurred when a child had a pocket full of fire-crackers. A spark managed to set them off resulting in serious burns to his thigh and penis. Fireworks are very dangerous in untrained hands.

- Many cities and towns have organized fireworks displays; these are the safest and the most spectacular. Watch the papers or TV for information about fireworks in your area.

- Check with the local fire department about setting off fireworks; there might be a ban on them in your area. Remember that fireworks can start fires.

- If you are going to light your own fireworks, read the instructions carefully and use common sense. Keep your children and bystanders a safe distance from the fireworks and don't set fire to the neighborhood.

Farm and Acreage Safety

21

In 1981 there were 16 fatal injuries to children on Alberta farms. That number has dropped to six or less per year since 1982. However, there are hundreds of serious injuries every year on farms and acreages. A reason for the reduction in injuries is the Alberta Farm Safety program. Check with your provincial or state agriculture departments for similar programs.

In rural settings, children face many of the same dangers that children growing up in the city face, but they are also exposed to the dangers of a potentially hazardous industrial setting.

On the farm or on an acreage, children must be instructed in safe practices from the time they are able to comprehend directions. In particular, you must set a good example; children will imitate you. This is yet another good example of where practising safety teaches safety!

If you live in a rural area it is very important to know which ambulance or fire department you will call in case of an emergency. You should be able to explain precisely how to get to your farm or acreage. Explaining that you live in the second purple house off the road is not much help to the emergency crews when it is two a.m. and raining. Because of poor directions, I have driven many needless miles and wasted much precious time on country roads looking for the people who called us.

In the U.S.A. approximately 300 children die and 24,000 sustain serious injuries on the nation's farms every year. A National Safety Council survey found children aged 5 to 14 were two-thirds more likely to suffer a farm work accident than adults aged 45 to 64 (Wisconsin Agriculturist, July 3, 1990).

A serious farm injury happened while I was writing this book. A tractor was pulling a cultivator, and an adult was driving the tractor with a ten year-old child riding on the tractor. A branch knocked the child off the machine and the child's leg was caught in and amputated by the cultivator.

Heavy equipment, livestock, dangerous chemicals, and water dugouts are but a few of the dangers that farm children face. Review a few of these observations and make sure your child's farm or acreage experience is safe. Two important preliminary ideas for farm and acreage safety are to:

- Devote a day for family safety instructions and rules;

- Designate a safe area for children, fenced in and well away from farm machinery and animals.

1. Farm Machines, Tools and Equipment Safety

- Children should always be supervised by a responsible adult around farm machinery, tools, and equipment.

- Never assume your children will naturally understand how to handle himself safely around machinery. You have the experience; they don't. Safety must be explained constantly.

- Don't allow children as extra riders on equipment. Many children and adults have been killed when they fell off moving machinery and were crushed under the wheels or run over by the equipment they were pulling.

- Do not allow children to operate machinery without a proper safety orientation.

- When running machinery, make sure you know where your children are; many children have been killed or injured when the operator has run them over. Walk around your machine(s) before starting them up.

- Leave any equipment that might fall — such as front-end loaders — in the down position.

- When self-propelled machinery is parked, brakes should be locked and keys removed from the ignition. *Never leave the keys in any farm machinery.*

- Teach children to stay completely away from power take offs on machinery.

- Keep machinery in good repair. Make sure all guards and shields are kept in place.

- All electrical wiring should be kept in good repair. Teach your children at an early age what electricity does and how dangerous it can be. Explain the dangers of overhead wires.

- Install locking devices on electrical equipment.

- Incidents involving tractors are the most common cause of child mortality in the farm environment. Such injuries are often related to the inexperience of the operator, although all too often tractors are the cause of death for even experienced farmers.

- Drive your tractor cautiously, being sure that all children are well out of the way.

- Tractor roll-overs are the most common type of mishap. Safety instruction must be given to any child who is old enough to operate machinery.

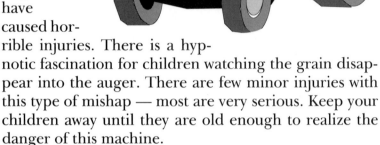

- Augers have caused horrible injuries. There is a hypnotic fascination for children watching the grain disappear into the auger. There are few minor injuries with this type of mishap — most are very serious. Keep your children away until they are old enough to realize the danger of this machine.

- Firearms are fairly common on a farm. Extreme care must be taken with the storage of guns. Instruct your children at an early age of the dangers of guns and have them take an approved safety course.

During the time this book was being written, an eight year-old girl was shot in the face by an older cousin who had taken the gun from the father's room.

Guns should never be stored loaded. Keep them in a locked area or cabinet. Ammunition should be stored in a locked area away from the gun. Keep the keys out of children's reach. They should be stored unloaded and the bullets should be stored separately. A trigger lock can reduce the chance of a dangerous situation.

2. Chemicals and Fuel Safety

- Make sure children will not be able to gain access to your gas and diesel storage tanks.

- Keep chemicals in a safe place.

3. Water Hazards

- Fence farm ponds, manure and silage pits to keep children out.

- If your children skate on dugouts or ponds, make sure the ice is thick enough to support their weight.

- Uncovered openings to septic tanks and wells have resulted in fatalities because children have fallen into them. Make sure it is impossible for your children to move the cover to expose the opening. A sheet of plywood is not an acceptable cover because it is too easy for children to remove it.

- It is common for people without children to overlook these hazards. If you are visiting a farm or acreage, inquire if your host has covered all water hazards. Make sure your children are kept away from these hazards.

4. Livestock

- Many deaths are attributed to livestock. Extreme care must be taken around animals.

- Supervise your children around animals. Sick animals or nursing animals can be particularly sensitive to quick movements or unexpected visitors. Teach your children how and when to approach a farm animal.

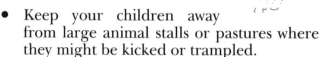

- When visiting, ask the owners for special instructions regarding the animals on the farm or acreage.

- Keep your children away from large animal stalls or pastures where they might be kicked or trampled.

- Teach children respect for all animals. And remember to set a good example yourself — your child will be watching you and will imitate your conduct around animals.

Day Care and Baby Sitters

22

1. Safety in Day Care Centres

More and more children spend a good part of their days in day care centers. Many parents trust that the children they put into a day care center will be safe. Unfortunately, day cares do not come with universal standards for care and safety — and when it comes to safety, there are no guarantees. Each province and state has different standards for licensed day care facilities and it is your responsibility as a consumer to be familiar with the legal status of day cares in your location.

As a parent or guardian, it is your responsibility to select and ensure the day care service is a safe and healthy environment for your child. Visit several centers well in advance of sending your child to a day care or family day home. Obtain written information about the law and child care facilities in your province or state. In Alberta, for example, licensed day care and family day homes come under the jurisdiction of Alberta Family and Social Services. They have regional offices throughout the province. Publications from this government agency are thorough and informative and will assist you in making child care decisions.

Day care injuries are frequently associated with playground equipment. Most of these injuries involve falls. See Chapter Fifteen, Playgrounds, for a discussion of playground safety.

Make sure that your child's day care playground follows the guidelines listed there.

In this section, I am primarily concerned with safety in the day care setting. The Alberta Family and Social Services pamphlet, "Choosing a Day Care Center: A Guide for Parents," lists some important health and safety concerns that you should look for in a day care. These concerns are a general guideline for evaluating most day care centers and family day homes. Here are a few of their excellent suggestions to ask yourself about your child's day care setting:

- Is your first impression of the day care setting that it is bright, cheerful, organized, and fresh and clean, with pleasant, spacious, warm, and inviting rooms? Are the children in the center busy and happily interested in activities?

- Do the staff members seem to be involved, caring, happy, and knowledgeable?

- Is the day care license posted in a conspicuous place and are recent inspection reports available for viewing?

- Is the setting clean and safe, with locked cupboards for cleaning products and other hazardous materials?

Day Care, Safe Care

- Are safety devices such as fire extinguishers, smoke detectors, and covers for electrical outlets evident and in good working order?

- Can you clearly see a posted list of emergency evacuation procedures and a designated relocation site, as well as emergency numbers posted near the telephone?

- Does the center have emergency exits that are easily reached and opened? The supervisor should be able to show you a record of fire drills; are drills held regularly?

- Current medical records must be kept by staff on each child in the case of emergency, including lists of children with allergies. Have the staff show you that medications are stored in a locked container inaccessible to children and that they have a record of medications given to children that is signed by parents. Parents should be required to give written permission for the administration of all medication.

- Do staff members have training in first aid and CPR for child care? Is there at least one staff member with a valid first aid and CPR certificate on the premises at all times?

- What are the procedures in case of accident or illness? Are the parents notified immediately? Are ill children supervised in a separate area and removed as quickly as possible?

- Has the staff kept current records for children's medical history, family and emergency contact numbers, and the names of people who are allowed to pick your child up from the center?

- Does the center have adequate protection on stairs and low windows? The center should have non-skid floors that are carpeted in areas such as the block center and book center.

*A survey carried out in one state found that even well-edu-
cated employees of a health care facility did not check their
child's day care setting for such important concerns as health
and safety features. Some of the parents tolerated unsafe conditions such as knowing that poisons and medications were
not kept locked up. About 70% of these parents reported that
there were unprotected drugs and or chemicals kept in the
bathroom.*

- Are there "sign-in" procedures so that staff know which children are present at all times? What is the day care's policy for authorizing the departure of a child with a designated adult or older sibling?

- Are children being taught basic hygiene, such as washing their hands after using the toilet? Do staff wash hands before and after each diaper change?

- Are there strict sanitary procedures for changing diapers and for toilet training, and are children with soiled diapers or pants being changed immediately?

- Change tables should be washed and disinfected before and after each diaper change and, similarly, potty chairs should be disinfected after each use.

- Does the center have clean clothes kept on hand for each child in case of "accidents"?

- Are nutritious meals that follow Canada's Food Guide offered, and are the menus posted weekly and followed?

- Is the kitchen off limits to children as a play space, except for special supervised activities?

- Is there a smoking ban in all areas of the day care center, including the playground?

- Does the center have liability insurance coverage for on and off-site activities? What are the supervision arrangements when children are being transported and is a parent's written approval required?

- What is the center's policy on discipline and is corporal punishment prohibited? How are problems or difficult behavior handled and how is the discipline policy communicated to the parents and staff?

These are only some of the guidelines that parents and guardians should be concerned with in selecting and contracting day care for their children. How can you be sure policies, regulations, and practices are being carried out consistently? Well, you can't, short of being on-site every day your child is in the program. However, you can be vigilant, ask questions frequently, and be involved as a volunteer whenever you can. Always feel free to drop in on a day care or family home care unannounced and to ask to observe at any time. In short, it is important to keep track of your child's situation to make sure it continues to be a good arrangement. Health and safety are primary concerns. Therefore, as a result of both your primary responsibility as your child's caregiver, and your daily visits to the center, you are in the best position to monitor the care given to your child.

2. Baby Sitters

Selecting an appropriate sitter to trust with the care and safety of your child is the key to providing children with proper care when parents cannot be at home. Pick a sitter carefully. Ideally, you will select someone you already know and trust. If this is not possible, ask for references.

Sitters come in all ages and levels of experience, but here are a few pointers for selecting an appropriate person to care for your precious child in your absence:

- Parents should consider the length of time and the time of day when the sitter will work, along with the ages and number of children who will be in the sitter's care. For some situations, an older teen or a mature adult may be the best choice.

- A sitter should be old enough and mature enough to handle the many responsibilities in the care and safety of your child. Baby-sitters should be at least twelve years old. Some twelve year-olds may be emotionally immature. By the same token, an older, more mature sitter should be alert, mobile, and responsible.

- When using a young sitter, ensure that he or she has taken a baby-sitting course. These courses require that the student be at least twelve years old. Generally, a thirteen year-old is capable of sitting for a few hours in an evening.

- When you require a sitter, you should select one well in advance of the first time you require her services. Don't wait until the last minute to contract a sitter. It will take the sitter a little time to become familiar with your children and house.

- Interview the potential sitter well before you need them. Watch to to see how they interact with your children.

- You should not expect a sitter to feel comfortable after a five minute briefing. Have the sitter over before you will actually need him so he can meet the children and you will have ample time to show him around the house and explain to him what you expect.

- Tell any sitter (including friends or grandparents) what you expect for child safety.

- Tour the house with your sitter, pointing out possible hazards, special features, such as stairways to be kept locked, or areas that are "off-limits" for your child.

- Get a list of references from other families your sitter has worked for and don't be shy about checking out those references. A reference should indicate a proven record of good judgment, maturity, and the ability to follow house rules and directions.

- After you have tried out a sitter, don't forget to ask the child how she liked the experience. Sometimes children can alert us to situations in which they feel threatened or uncomfortable.

Many cities and towns have baby-sitting courses. These courses provide the sitters insights into the responsibilities of baby-sitting. Course topics usually range from basic child and infant care to what to do in case of a fire. Even if the sitter has taken such a course, discuss with her the following points:

- Provide the sitter with a clear list of where you are going and how you can be contacted in case of an emergency. (If you have a cellular phone, you can be reached almost anywhere.) Don't feel shy about calling home just to "check in" — and certainly call if your plans change and you will be in a different location.

- Make sure you have an emergency phone list and the sitter knows that it is posted by your phone. The list should begin with the full address and phone number of your home (in case the sitter is not familiar with it). Then include: Emergency 911 and/or the police, the local fire department and ambulance service, the local poison control center, where the parents can be reached, a nearby friend or relative, and the family doctor or pediatrician.

- Directions to the sitter should include house rules, what allergies the children have, what the children may eat, when bed time is, and the appropriate manner of discipline. A primary instruction should be that the children should never be left alone, not even for a minute.

- Instruct the sitter to never give medication to the children unless they are instructed to do so by you. If you wish them to administer medication, make sure they know how to give it and how much to give and when to give it.

- Instruct the sitter in the use of all baby products and equipment. Make sure instructions for using the security system, stereo equipment, microwave and the stove are clear.

- Sitters need to know how to handle minor emergencies, including basic first aid; they should know where the first aid kit is in your home. Sitters should know where the flashlight is in case of a power outage.

- Show your sitter what exits to use in case of fire. (See Escape Plan in *Burns and Scalds,* Chapter Six) Instruct her to get the children out and not to go back in, and to have a neighbor phone the fire department.

- Smoke detectors should be in good working order and the sitter should know the locations of your fire extinguishers.

- The sitter should know how the doors lock, where the keys are kept, and how to get out of the house in an emergency.

- The doors must be kept locked at all times and never opened for strangers. It is generally recommended that your friends and the sitter's should not come to visit. Distractions could mean that the sitter is not paying attention to your child.

- Should a person unknown to the sitter telephone your home, ask the sitter to take a message. She should not let the caller know that she is alone with the children. A telephone answering machine can be used to screen calls. Develop a policy for telephone use with your sitter prior to hiring.

- Instruct your sitter on what to do if someone knocks on the door. Be sure to alert the sitter to any callers or deliveries that you are expecting when you are gone.

- Remind baby sitters not to be afraid to call for help for any reason.

- Give a copy of *Kids for Keeps* to your sitter to read after the children are asleep and let her keep it as "tip" above and beyond her pay the first time you hire her.

Personal Safety 23

I t is a common perception that children face more dangers growing up than their parents had to face. Missing children, child abuse, sexual assaults, and child homicides are all too frequently the subject on TV news or in the newspaper. There is no foolproof way to protect your children from all the dangers in the world unless you lock them in sterile rooms and never let them out. Awareness, training, and care can protect you and your child from some of the harsher realities of the world.

1. Sexual Abuse

Unfortunately, sexual abuse is a reality in our contemporary society. Some children are sexually abused every year and the problem can be difficult to detect, because — in many cases — the child knows the abuser. Here are some guidelines to teach your children how to avoid the danger of child abuse. From *Safe & Secure: A Guide to Prevention of Injuries to Preschoolers:*

- Teach your child "Stranger Awareness." By three and four years, a child can be taught the difference between a stranger and a trusted friend or family member.

- Use a family secret code word — your child will know to go only with adults who use that word.

- Teach your child that nobody has the right to touch the areas of their body covered by a bathing suit. Tell them to say "no" to any person who tries to touch them in this way and that on this occasion it is perfectly acceptable to say "no" to an adult. Teach them to let you know if someone has tried to touch them inappropriately.

- Teach your children to run home or to the nearest Block Parent's home if someone is following or frightening them.

2. Abduction

When a child is missing it is a parent's worst nightmare. Authorities tell us that in 87% of these cases the child is abducted by a non-custodial parent. Further, "run-aways" account for 75% of all missing children. Stranger abductions are less common, but they also happen. These figures are not meant to scare you, but they should put a perspective on the abduction of children. Rather than live in fear of an abduction, empower your child with viable strategies and responses to uncomfortable situations.

A little training could help reduce the risk of abduction and increase your child's safety. Here are some tips to teach your child about personal safety adapted from The Story of Ruby and Watchdog, A Guide to Your Child's Personal Safety, a brochure published by Alberta Solicitor General, Law Enforcement Division.

A. What Your Children Should Know

- Your child should know his or her full name, age, telephone number (including area code), city, province, or state and how to make local, collect, and long distance telephone calls. Practice these skills with your child routinely.

- Remember your secret code word. Never tell anyone your secret word. Never believe strangers who say your parents sent them to pick you up — unless they know the code word.

- Whenever possible your children should walk and play with other children. Avoid unsupervised playgrounds or deserted areas where a stranger could approach them unobserved.

- Don't go to washrooms or out-of-the-way places unless an adult you know is with you.

- Children should refuse gifts or rides from strangers. If approached they should run away, making as much noise as possible. Instruct them to try to remember the stranger's description, what his motor vehicle looked like, and, if possible, the license plate number.

- Yell for help and fight if anyone tries to hurt you or make you go with them.

- Should a stranger threaten them, teach children to seek the safety of a home, a Block Parent, or the nearest public place such as a store, an office, or a restaurant.

- If children are home alone, they should not open the door without identifying the callers, either visually through a window or peephole in the door, or by the use of a password known only to those who can be trusted.

- Don't tell anyone on the phone that your parents are not at home. Just say that they can't come to the phone right now and take a message.

- Tell your parents or another adult you know if anyone has been following you or approached you in a way that makes you feel uncomfortable. Never be afraid to tell.

B. What You Should Know

- Give the school, day care center and any caregiver for your child the names of persons to whom your child may be released. Always provide phone numbers where you can be reached in an emergency.

- Remember what your child was wearing each day in case he does not return. Write your child's name somewhere on her clothing where it will not be easily seen. A child is less likely to fear a stranger who knows his name; avoid clothing and accessories that have your child's name printed on them.

- Keep an up-to-date record of your child, including a recent photograph, the child's height, weight, medical and dental histories, and, if possible a video tape and finger print record. These are important tools in finding lost children.

- Interview potential baby sitters and always follow up on their references. (See Chapter Twenty Two, *Day Care and Baby-sitters.*)

- Know the phone numbers and addresses of your child's friends; and insist that your child asks permission before they go play with friends. Confirm the details of the visit with the parents of the child's friends.

- Accompany your child everywhere and do not let them loiter in public places — especially in or near public washrooms.

- Listen to your children! Take seriously their accounts of people who make them uncomfortable.

C. What You Should Do If Your Child Is Missing

Try to stay calm, even though this is probably the most stressful time a parent can endure. Search your home and surrounding areas. Check with playmates, neighbors, and relatives, and in favorite play areas. Contact the police and be prepared to give the following information:

- full physical description;
- birth marks or other identification marks;
- most recent photograph;
- fingerprint record card;
- description of clothing worn at time of disappearance;
- medical problems;
- recent problems at home, school, with playmates, etc.;
- possible or probable abduction by spouse, former spouse or relative;
- assessment of possible runaway, because favorite clothes and possessions are missing.

3. Adult Anger and The Shaken Baby Syndrome

In November, 1991, an eighteen year-old man shook a seven week-old infant whom he was baby-sitting because he wanted him to stop crying. The infant died the next day.

Jamie had been crying for hours. I felt like I could shake the life out of her. A moment later, I had (a quotation from a mother).

Normal babies will cry two to three hours per day. They cry if they are hungry, need to be changed, or want to be picked up. There are times when even the most calm and relaxed person will feel very stressed and feel like she is unable to cope with a crying child. If there are other stresses in the household, these feelings can be magnified. Sometimes — out of great frustration — a caregiver picks up a baby and will shake it. Because the baby's head is heavier and larger in comparison to the rest of the body, and the neck muscles are not fully developed, the head moves rapidly and unnaturally in a back-and-forth motion. The brain hits the inside of the skull. This can cause permanent brain damage.

Guard well your baby's precious head,
Shake, jerk and slap it never,
Lest you bruise his brain and twist his mind,
or whiplash him dead forever (Dr. John Caffey).

Never Shake - Walk Away

A few tips you can use to help deal with a crying baby are:

- Never shake a baby.

- Learn how to soothe your baby. Seek the help of professionals if you are having difficulty with this.

- Be patient — walk away; count to ten and take a deep breath.

- Learn a relaxation technique.

- Find a friend, especially one with children, to confide in — friends often have had similar experiences.

- Take a break and have someone else look after the baby.

- Learn about the child's development.

- Deal with issues of family violence.

Kids for Keeps

Conclusion

I realize that reading this book was not exactly light entertainment. What could be more serious than the safety of your children? I know there are hundreds of parents and other caregivers who would have given anything to have learned and understood the hazards discussed in this book by reading about them, rather than learning about them by first hand experience. The parents of those children loved their children as much as I love mine, or you love yours. They just didn't realize the dangers.

After reading *Kids for Keeps*, you are now aware of many of the hazards that are found around the home and elsewhere in your child's environment. It is not enough just to be aware of the hazards; you must eliminate these dangers. Look at your environment from a child's point of view. Get down on your hands and knees, and look at things as a child sees them. Find the hazards and remove them, fix them, get them picked up! This should not be a chore, but just another way of expressing your love for your child.

Martin Lesperance, 1995

Appendix

A

Further Reading

Albers Hill, Barbara, and Audrey Talkington. *To Save a Child*. Avery Publishing Group Inc. 1993.

Lansky, Vicki. *A Parent's Guide to Child Safety*. Safety First, 1991.

McKay, Sharon E. *The New Child Safety Handbook*. Macmillan of Canada, 1988.

Miller, Jeanne E. *The Perfectly Safe Home*. Simon and Schuster, 1991.

Appendix B

Safety Resources

Farm Safety Program

Farm Safety Association
Alberta Agriculture 340 Woodlawn Road W.
201 J.G. O'Donoghue Building Suite 22-23
Edmonton, Alberta T6H 5T6

Product Safety Bureau, Health Canada (formerly Consumer and
Corporate Affairs, Canada) Headquarters-Ottawa/Hull (819)
953-8082

For Information on Safe Toys

Canadian Toy Testing Council
#105, 17 York Street 950 Gladstone Ave., Suite 110
Ottawa, Ontario K1N 5S7
(613) 238-8425 (613) 729-7101

CAA Child Restraint Information Offices

Canadian Automobile Association
1775 Courtwood Crescent
Ottawa, Ontario K2C 3J2
Telephone 613- 226-7631

British Columbia Automobile Association	(604) 298-2122
Alberta Motor Association (Edmonton)	(403) 430-6800
Alberta Motor Association	(800) 222-6578
CAA Saskatchewan	(800) 667-3319
Manitoba Motor League	(204) 987-6176
CAA Thunder Bay	(807) 345-1261
CAA Northeastern Ontario	(705) 522-0000
CAA Toronto	(416) 964-3170
Hamilton Automobile Club	(416) 525-1210
CAA Mid-Western Ontario	(519) 894-2582
CAA Elgin Norfolk Club	(519) 631-6490
CAA Niagara	(416) 688-0321
CAA Windsor	(519) 542-3493
CAA Peterborough	(705) 743-4343
CAA Eastern Ontario	(613) 546-2596
CAA Ottawa	(613) 820-1890
CAA Quebec	(418) 624-2424
CAA Maritimes	(506) 634-1400
Newfoundland	(800) 561-8807
Your Local CAA Club Office	

Kids for Keeps

Other Organizations

Safe Kids Canada
1300, 180 Dundas Street, West
Toronto, Ontario M5G 1Z8

Safe Kids is an excellent program which has very good information on a variety of child injuries and how to prevent them. Much of the information in this book was taken from their handouts.

Infant and Toddler Safety Association
385 Fairway Road South, Suite 4A-230
Kitchener, Ontario N2C 2N9
(519) 570-0181

This is a non-profit, volunteer organization which gives workshops and publishes a newsletter that comes with a minimal membership fee. The newsletter gives excellent information on hazards to children and how to help prevent injuries.

The Canadian Institute of Child Health
Suite 512, 885 Meadowlands Drive E.
Ottawa, Ontario K2C 3N2
(613) 224-4144

This non-profit organization believes that children have a right to enjoy the best state of health possible. Among their many goals is the promotion of a healthy and safe environment and the incidence reduction of childhood injuries.

University of Alberta Hospitals
Injury Prevention Centre
4075 Educational Development Centre
8308 114 Street
Edmonton, Alberta T6G 2P7
(403) 492-6019

This organization produces a newsletter which covers many different topics on injury prevention not only for children but for all ages.

**Life Support Training of
Grant MacEwan Community College**
offers all levels of Heart & Stroke Foundation CPR as well as all levels of Medic First Aid. Specific courses relating to children include:

- Infant/Child CPR

- Pediatric First Aid

- Caregiver First Aid

For further information on courses or to order additional copies of "*Kids for Keeps*", please contact:

Life Support Training
Grant MacEwan Community College
7319-29 Avenue
Edmonton, Alberta, Canada T6K 2P1
(403) 497-4010

For more information about CPR in your province, contact your local Heart and Stroke Foundation.

Appendix

Harmful Products

Harmful products which may be found in or around the home.

Acid or alkalis	Lead from pencils, paints or other products
Adhesives such as glues or epoxies	Lighter fluid — liquid or gas types
Aerosol cans	Lye
Alcohol — rubbing or drinking	Medications
Ammonia	Metal furniture
Aspirin	Mothballs
Bath oils or beads	Mouthwash
Batteries	Nail polish remover
Birth-control pills	Oils and grease
Bleach	Oven cleaner
Cayenne pepper	Paint thinner and strippers
Cigarettes and cigar tobacco or butts	Paints and varnishes
Cleaning supplies (all types)	Pet food and medicines
Cosmetics Wax — floor or automobile	Plants
Detergent — clothes or dishwasher	Polishes, such as for shoes
Drain cleaner	Razor blades
Felt tip markers	Rug and spot cleaner
Fertilizers	Shampoo
Furniture polish	Soaps
Gasoline	Suntan lotion
Herbicides	Swimming pool and hot tub chemicals
Inks	Toilet cleaner
Insulation	Toothpicks
Iron pills	Turpentine
Laxatives	Vitamins
	Water softener pellets

Appendix

D

After you have read this book, please walk through the different rooms in your home and see if there are any hazards to your children. This is just a partial list; please refer to the pertinent chapters in the book for a more detailed list of hazards.

Listed below are some questions you should ask yourself as you look through your home. Fill out the checklist and see if the rooms can be made safer.

Have you taken a Cardiopulmonary Resuscitation (CPR) and First Aid course?

Safety Check

The Kitchen

☐ When you cook, do you keep the pot handles turned in?

☐ Are children kept at a safe distance when you are cooking?

☐ Do you keep knives and other sharp utensils in a safe place?

☐ Are electrical appliances kept in a safe place? Can the electrical cords be reached by children?

☐ Are children left unattended on counters, even for a short time?

☐ Do you keep drain cleaners, oven cleaners and dishwasher detergent in a safe place?

☐ Have you installed child proof locks on cupboards?

☐ Is there an appliance latch on the fridge?

☐ Are medications kept on the kitchen table or any other accessible area?

☐ Do you leave buckets of water in the kitchen, that a child can fall into?

☐ Are you prepared for a fire in the kitchen if one happens?

☐ Is there a safety gate to stop children from falling down the stairs to the basement?

☐ Do you have emergency phone numbers, such as fire and police, posted close to the phone?

☐ Is the highchair a safe one, and is it used in a safe manner?

☐ Could a child bring everything on the table down onto his head by pulling on the tablecloth?

☐ Are there socket guards on electrical outlets?

☐ Is the garbage in a locked cupboard?

☐ Are the garbage and other plastic bags kept in a safe place?

The Bathroom

☐ Could you get into the bathroom if your child locked himself in?

☐ Is there a lock on the toilet lid?

☐ Are medications and other potentially dangerous products kept in a safe place?

Kids for Keeps

- ☐ Do you keep razors and other dangerous products in a safe place?

- ☐ Are appliances such as hairdryers unplugged when not in use?

- ☐ Are there harmful things in the garbage can that could be reached by children?

- ☐ Do you have a non-slip surface in your bathtub?

- ☐ Are the faucets in the bathtub padded in case of a fall?

- ☐ Have you checked the temperature of the hot water to ensure that it will not scald (48 degrees C., 120 degrees F).

The Child's Room

- ☐ Is the crib safe? Does it meet current safety standards?

- ☐ Is there anything in or around the crib that could cause harm to your child?

- ☐ Are socket guards in place? Do you have a safe night light?

- ☐ Are there blind cords that can be reached by your children?

- ☐ Is the toy box safe? Could your child get in and suffocate? Could the lid fall down and hurt him?

- ☐ Does the bed have a guard to keep children from slipping between the bed and the wall?

- ☐ If you have bunkbeds, are they safe? Are they strong and sturdy. Do they have a safe ladder and guards to help prevent falls?

- ☐ Is there a dresser that a child could pull down on himself by standing on the lower drawers?

Living Room

☐ Are cords for drapes and blinds kept out of reach?

☐ Do you keep bowls of nuts, small candies etc. out of reach of small children?

☐ Is the carpet kept clear of small objects that a child could choke on?

☐ Is there a reclining chair that could close on small children?

☐ Are sharp corners on furniture and the fireplace hearth padded?

☐ Is there a fireplace screen and is the gas key kept in a safe place?

☐ If you have a glass coffee table, is it fitted with safety glass?

☐ Are the electrical outlets protected with socket guards?

☐ Do you regularly check your smoke detectors?

☐ Do you keep the alcohol cabinet locked?

☐ Is the gun cabinet locked and ammunition kept in a separate place?

☐ Are there poisonous plants in the house? Can the non poisonous plants be reached and the leaves choked on?

Bibliography

Books

McKay, Sharon E.
The New Child Safety Handbook,
   Canada: Macmillan, 1988

Miller, Jeanne
The Perfectly Safe Home.
   New York: Simon and Schuster, 1991

Lansky, Vicki
A Parents Guide to Child Safety. A Comprehensive Handbook from Crib to Preschool.
   Deephaven, MN: Safety First, 1991

Talkington, Audrey E. and Barbara Albers Hill
To Save a Child. Things You Can Do to Protect, Nurture and Teach Our Children.
   Garden City, NY: Avery, 1993

Magazines

Alberta Safe Kids and Alberta Medical Association

Removing Playground Hazards for our Children's Sake - a Resource Kit for Alberta Communities.
   Published by The Rotary Club of St. Albert. April 1993

University of Alberta Hospitals

Injury Prevention News. University of Alberta Hospitals: Edmonton Vol. 3, no 10, November/December 1990

Injury Prevention News. University of Alberta Hospitals: Edmonton Vol. 6, no 7, November/December 1993

Infant and Toddler Safety Association

Grow Safely A News Letter for Families of Young Children Vol. 2, no 2, June 1987

Grow Safely A News Letter for Families of Young Children Vol. 3, no 1, Spring 1988

Grow Safely A News Letter for Families of Young Children Vol. 4, no 3, September 1989

Grow Safely A News Letter for Families of Young Children Vol. 5, no 4, December 1990

Grow Safely A News Letter for Families of Young Children Vol. 6, no 2, June 1992

Grow Safely A News Letter for Families of Young Children Vol. 9, no 3, Fall 1994

Booklets, Pamphlets and Fact Sheets

Canadian Paediatric Society, Ross Laboratories
Keep Your Child Safe. Canada. 1989

Alberta Safe Kids Campaign: Fact Sheet
Home Safety Checklist, Summer Time and the Burning is Easy.

Alberta Safe Kids Campaign: Information Sheet
How to Choose and Use Baby Strollers. 1988

Transport Canada: Booklet
Keep Them Safe. A Guide to Children's Car Seats. Transport Canada. 1993

Edmonton Board of Health

Child/Passenger-Related Bicycle Injuries
Childhood Injury Control Newsletter (CHIC) No. 1.4

Dangers of Baby Walkers
Childhood Injury Control Newsletter (CHIC) No. 2.3

Pet Ferrets-A Hazard to Infants and Children
Childhood Injury Control Newsletter (CHIC) No. 2.4

Biting Mosquitos and Children
Childhood Injury Control Newsletter (CHIC) No. 2.5

Sparks, Blazes and Burns-Cigarette Lighters and Child Fireplay
Childhood Injury Control Newsletter (CHIC) No. 2.6

Tobogganing and Sledding Injuries
Childhood Injury Control Newsletter (CHIC) No. 3.1

Trampoline-Related Injuries
Childhood Injury Control Newsletter (CHIC) No. 3.3

Christmas Safety
Childhood Injury Control Newsletter (CHIC) No. 3.4

Dog Bite Injuries
Childhood Injury Control Newsletter (CHIC) No. 4.2

Window Blind Cords
Childhood Injury Control Newsletter (CHIC) No. 4.4

Injuries Associated with Choking
Childhood Injury Control Newsletter (CHIC) No. 4.5

Injuries Associated with In-Line Skating
Childhood Injury Control Newsletter (CHIC) No. 5.3

The Prevention of Drownings in Preschoolers
Childhood Injury Control Newsletter (CHIC) No. 6.4

Injuries to a Shaken Baby
Childhood Injury Control Newsletter (CHIC) No. 6.5

Basic Life Support Resource
Heart and Stroke Foundation of Canada

INDEX

Index   213

Kids for Keeps

Index   215

Index   217

The author has a slide presentation based on the book *Kids for Keeps* which deals with hazards that are found around the home, yard and playground. This dynamic and informative presentation can be adapted in length to meet your company's safety meetings.

Martin Lesperance is also available for keynote presentations which deal with child safety and home safety with examples of actual emergency situations he has attended. These presentations encompass both the humorous and the serious aspects of Emergency Medical Services.

For more information:

Call (403) 225-2011 or Fax (403) 932-7674

Mailing Address:

Box 1769, Cochrane, Alberta, Canada T0L 0W0

To order additional copies of *Kids for Keeps:*

Call: 1-800-601-3852

(Inquire about Volume Discount)